Be A Bean!

Life Lessons for Anyone & Everyone Who Wants to Live a Good Life, Be a Better Leader, and Change the World

Keith G. Feit, Ph.D.

Copyright © 2017 KGF Partners, Inc.

All rights reserved.

ISBN: 197927066x
ISBN-13: 978-1979270663

DEDICATION

This book is dedicated to the memory of Dr. John Pisapia, my dissertation chair, mentor, and close friend. He lives on in all my work... his words continue to inspire me, his lessons continue to guide my journey, and his influence continues to define who I am as a leader.

TABLE OF CONTENTS

THE PARABLE (THE LEADERSHIP INSPIRATION):
CARROTS, EGGS, AND COFFEE BEANS, 1

INTRODUCTION, 3

LESSON #1: A LEADER'S GOLDEN RULE - POSITIVE IMPACT, 5

LESSON #2: MAKE A DIFFERENCE, DON'T BE A WITNESS, 13

LESSON #3: IGNORE THE WHISPERS, 19

LESSON #4: IT TAKES A TEAM…, 25

LESSON #5: CHASE PERFECTION, ACHIEVE EXCELLENCE, 29

LESSON #6: SPEAK TO HOPE, NOT FEAR, 33

LESSON #7: CELEBRATE FAILURE, 37

LESSON #8: BE THE MASTER OF YOUR FATE, 43

LESSON #9: PAINT IN BOLD COLORS, NOT PALE PASTELS, 49

LESSON #10: SHAVE THE DARN BIRD!, 55

LESSON #11: CHANGE THE RULES, 59

LESSON #12: ASK NOT WHAT YOUR FOLLOWERS CAN DO FOR YOU…, 65

LESSON #13: THE ONLY THING YOU HAVE TO FEAR…, 71

LESSON #14: KNOW WHEN TO LEAD AND WHEN TO FOLLOW, 77

LESSON #15: CHALLENGES – BARRIERS, OBSTACLES, OR OPPORTUNITIES?, 81

LESSON #16: RELATIONSHIPS RULE, 87

LESSON #17: "LITTLE" WINS EQUAL "BIG" LIFE, 91

LESSON #18: EMBRACE ADVERSITY, 95

LESSON #19: LEARN FROM THE PAST, LIVE IN THE PRESENT, CREATE THE FUTURE, 101

LESSON #20: A LEADER'S BEST FRIEND, 105

CULMINATING LESSON: ENJOY THE JOURNEY, 111

FEIT'S FINAL THOUGHTS…, 115

THE 10 COMMANDMENTS OF A LEADER, 117

ACKNOWLEDGMENTS

I would like to thank all those individuals who have helped me along my journey – my parents for their constant support, my grandfather for his inspiration, my friends for always being willing to listen (and always putting up with me), my professors for all the learning and mentoring, my colleagues for all their trust, respect, and support, and my students and players for all of their contributions to my leadership experiences.

Be a Bean is the first installment in a series of leadership books. The Feit Leadership Series will also include the future publications of *The Ten Commandments of a Leader; Burn the Boats, Build the Bridges;* and *A Meaningless Life*.

Be A Bean!

THE PARABLE

"Leadership and learning are indispensable to each other."
– President John F. Kennedy

A young woman went to her mother and told her about her life and how things were so hard for her. She did not know how she was going to make it and wanted to give up. She was tired of fighting and struggling. It seemed as one problem was solved another arose.

Her mother took her to the kitchen. She filled three pots with water.

In the First, she placed carrots, in the second she placed eggs, and the last she placed ground coffee beans. She let them sit and boil without saying a word.

In about twenty minutes she turned off the burners.

She fished the carrots out and placed them in a bowl. She pulled the eggs out and placed them in a bowl. Then she ladled the coffee out and placed it in a bowl.

Turning to her daughter, she asked, "Tell me, what do you see?"

"Carrots, eggs, and coffee," she replied.

She brought her closer and asked her to feel the carrots. She did and noted that they got soft. She then asked her to take and egg and break it. After pulling off the shell, she observed the hard-boiled egg. Finally, she asked her to sip the coffee. The daughter smiled as she tasted its rich aroma.

The daughter then asked, "What's the point, mother?"

Her mother explained that each of the objects had faced the same adversity—boiling water—but each reacted differently. The carrot went in strong, hard, and unrelenting. However, after being subjected to the boiling water, it softened and became weak. The egg had been fragile. Its thin outer shell had protected its liquid interior. But, after sitting through the boiling water, its inside became hardened.

The ground coffee beans were unique, however. After they were in the boiling water THEY HAD CHANGED THE WATER.

"Which are you?" she asked the daughter. "When adversity knocks on your door, how do you respond? Are you a carrot, an egg, or a coffee bean?"

Introduction

Leadership is a lot of things to a lot of people. Many different scholars and practitioners have differing definitions of leadership. However, there is no debate that leaders influence others. The question is – Where does the influence of the leader end? Does he or she influence only followers, or also those who do not support him or her? Does the leader influence the market, the community, the world, in general, or are his or her powers to impact relegated strictly to within the confines of the organization?

Remember the question the mother asked her daughter in the parable you just read. I ask you the same question. Who are you? Are you a carrot, softened by adversity, scared to challenge the environment even when you know it needs to be challenged? Are you an egg, hardened by adversity and so set in your ways that when the environment changes you fail to understand the changes as opportunities for a new beginning? Or are you a coffee bean, that refuses to let circumstance change you, that stands up to adversity, meets hardship head on, and changes the environment around you. Think of the people you know. Think of the leaders you have experienced. Think of those challenges in life when you had the choice to be a carrot, egg, or coffee bean. What did you choose?

The goal of every leader should be to be a bean. What does this mean? This means a leader should not only work to influence his or her followers, but also to influence the external environment. The leader should always work to be not merely a master of his or her organization, but a master of the market. He or she should endeavor to determine where the game will be played, control how the game will be played, and decide on the rules by which the game will be played. A bean does not allow the world outside to dictate the fate of the organization, but rather works so that the organization changes the world outside.

This book was written not as research. As you will see, it does not follow APA format, there are not loads of citations noting the research of various scholars. This is simply my roadmap to becoming a bean as a leader and in life. Each lesson has been taken from past learning and previous experiences, not from readings and studies. Michael Jordan, the greatest basketball player of all time, once said, "Earn your leadership every day." I believe these lessons make that a reality. This book is nothing more than, and is presented simply as, my philosophy on being an effective leader and a good person, and lessons I believe can lead anyone on a journey toward changing the world one person at a time.

Lesson #1
A LEADER'S GOLDEN RULE: POSITIVE IMPACT

"We make a living by what we get, but we make a life by what we give."
— Sir Winston Churchill

> *"I have an irrepressible desire to live till I can be assured the world is a little better for my having lived in it."*
> - President Abraham Lincoln

The quality of the life we lead, and in turn, the lives of those who follow us as leaders, will be determined by what we contribute to improving lives and society. As Churchill stated, what we give governs the life we make for ourselves. Life is a combination of our decisions and actions, and those decisions and actions affect not only us, but others, as well.

All leaders should strive to conduct themselves according to the words spoken by Abraham Lincoln in his second inaugural address, "…With malice toward none, with charity for all, with firmness in the right…" Be gracious in defeat, magnanimous in victory; always treat others, whether followers or competition, with respect and a kind heart. We all understand how our treatment

> *"Be ashamed to die until you have won some victory for humanity."*
> - Horace Mann

of those who stand by our sides has a tremendous impact on those individuals and our organization, but much is determined by how we treat those who stand against us. A leader's interactions with opposition can lead to both good and bad consequences. Lincoln had planned to move forward with a charitable re-assimilation of the confederates into the union after the Civil War. Despite much bad blood, Lincoln knew that malice and harsh treatment toward the southerners would only further divisions, lead to more violence, and delay the re-unification of the United States of America. One cannot have a positive impact without a charitable heart… malice in one's soul hinders a leader's ability to focus on the impact of his or her actions, rather than the immediate gratification of defeating one's enemy, gaining vengeance, or progressing at the expense of others.

Throughout life you will be faced with decisions, you will be in situations, you will find yourself face to face with a moment where the decision you make and the actions you take will profoundly impact the lives of others. Always be mindful of how what you do and what you say affects others. You never know how impactful your choice of words or the behaviors in which you partake may be for an individual struggling to cope with issues at home, work, or in his or her social life. What you say and do could be the difference between whether that individual successfully moves beyond his or her problems or falls prey to the pressures of adversity. That individual's success or failure does not occur in isolation and will certainly affect others, and so on. You could be the deciding factor in whether a chain of events and multitude of lives will be positive or negative, and whether those events and people will lead to a better world or a more troubled one.

There have been many leaders who have had a positive impact with large scale actions. There are some people who have the power to do that. Kings, queens, presidents, prime ministers, and other world leaders have the position, authority, and resources to influence millions in a positive manner. For example, in the

Be A Bean!

United States, President Abraham Lincoln emancipated the slaves in the 1860s, freeing millions of African Americans from bondage. One hundred years later, Martin Luther King, Jr. led a civil rights movement to provide rights to and improve the lives of those Black American men and women. Pope John Paul II and U.S. President Ronal Reagan fought communism in Eastern Europe in the 1980s, leading to the eventual fall of communism and the freeing of hundreds of millions of people from the tyranny of that oppressive economic and political system. U.S. President John F. Kennedy established the Peace Corps in the 1960s, helping to improve the lives of countless citizens of third world nations around the world.

> *"I've learned that people will forget what you said, people will forget what you did, but people will never forget how you made them feel."*
>
> - Maya Angelou, American Poet Laureate

Organizational leaders, for the most part, do not have quite that far-reaching influence, but they do have the ability to make a difference in the lives of those members of the organization and all those impacted by the efforts of the organizations, be it customers, clients, or community members. In the same way, team leaders have limited power to influence but can make a difference in the lives of every member of their team, and in turn the lives of the family members of each of those individuals. Positive impact is not reserved for those who have been appointed to prestigious positions or those who have found wealth and have seemingly unlimited resources. You do not have to be powerful or wealthy to positively influence someone's life.

The important thing to remember regarding positive impact is that you do not have to have been given anything to leave your mark on the lives of others. You can make the world a better place, and be a leader, without any formal acknowledgement of rank or positional authority. You can be powerless and impact those with power. You can be poor and impact those with wealth. Material power and wealth may often determine status, but it does not determine one's ability to lead and influence. ***We all influence the lives of others by every word we speak, every decision we make, and every action we take.*** You may be weak in rank, but strong in spirit. You may be poor of material wealth, but rich in heart. You are the one who determines the impact you have on the lives of others and the mark you leave on this world, one person at a time. Here is a parable that demonstrates how even the smallest of actions can make the largest of differences in the lives of others:

> *A wise man used to go to the ocean to do his writing. He had a habit of walking on the beach before he began his work. One day he was walking along the shore and looking down the beach, he saw a human figure moving like a dancer. He smiled to himself thinking of someone who would dance to the day. So he began to walk faster to catch up.*
>
> *As he got closer, he saw that it was a young man and the young man wasn't dancing, but instead he was reaching down to the shore, picking up something, and very gently throwing it into the ocean.*
>
> *As he got closer, he called out, "Good morning! What are you doing?"*
>
> *The young man paused, looked up, and replied, "Throwing starfish in the ocean."*
>
> *"I guess I should have asked, why are you throwing starfish in the ocean?"*
>
> *The young man replied, "The sun is up and the tide is going out. If I don't throw them in, they'll die."*
>
> *The wise man answered, "But, young man,*

Be A Bean!

don't you realize that there are miles and miles of beach and starfish all along it? You can't possibly make a difference!"

The young man listened politely. He then bent down, pick up another starfish, and threw it into the sea, past the breaking waves, and said, "It made a difference to that one.

Having a positive impact does not have to mean you are changing the world in one instance or by one act. If you improve the life of just one person, then you have had a positive impact. Every little act of kindness, every selfless action, every time you demonstrate compassion for others, you have had a positive impact. Even if it is only one little starfish you saved from drying up and dying, then you have made the world a little bit of a better place.

I look back on my life as a person and leader, and have some mixed analysis of my success. For nearly 20 years, I have been evaluated as a highly effective teacher, I have won many games and championships as a coach, and succeeded in building athletics programs and implementing initiatives that have helped improve my schools. I guess one can say that professionally, I have been a success, but through my eyes, these accomplishments are merely opportunities I have had to experience true success. I truly believe that my success depends on the lives of others. I always ask, "Have I made someone else's life better?" This is why I carry a card of Abraham Lincoln in my wallet. The quote on the back reads, "I have an irrepressible desire

> *"I expect to pass through life but once. If, therefore, there can be any kindness I can show, or any good thing I can do for any fellow being, let me do it now... as I shall not pass this way again."*
>
> - William Penn,
> Founder of Pennsylvania

to live until I can be assured that the world is a little better for my having lived in it." This card sits behind my license and is a constant reminder of why I do the things I do, say the things I say, and live the life I live. It reminds me that even if I am struggling to help myself, I can always do something, even the smallest of things, to help someone else.

The championship celebrations are fantastic, but those memories fade. A student telling me 15 years later that I profoundly impacted his or her life for the better is an achievement that lives on forever. The raise I get for a job well done allows me to spend a little more, but it does not provide me with the self-actualization I desire. However, using that money to help someone less fortunate brings me closer to being the person I want to be. I have failed in many aspects of life, especially in some of those things that are most important to me. I have disappointed many people, and have even on occasion unintentionally hurt those I love more than life itself. I have many regrets, but the one thing that drives me to continue, to overcome the disappointments, and to continue to help others, is the desire, that when I leave this world, I would have made a difference, even if for just one person.

As they say, Rome wasn't built in a day. The entirety of your positive impact will not present itself all at once, in a time of your choosing, or a manner of your liking. Often, you will never see the good that comes from your words or actions. Rest assured, however, that doesn't mean that your words and actions were not impactful. In fact, it is often in those times when we do not see a "return on our investment," so to speak, that we are having the most impact. As legendary Hall of Fame college basketball coach, John Wooden, once said, "The true test of man's character is what he does when no one is looking." Do not concern yourself with who sees the good you are doing, or if anyone at all is aware of the sacrifices you have made in an effort to positively impact those around you. Your only concern should be whether you have done all you could to leave the world a better place for having lived in it.

Be A Bean!

> **LESSON LEARNED:** *Every word you speak, every decision you make, and every action you take impacts the lives of others... be sure to always think of them, and think, speak, and behave in ways that improves lives, communities, and the world.*

Keith G. Feit

Lesson #2
MAKE A DIFFERENCE, DON'T BE A WITNESS

"Strong people stand up for themselves, but stronger people stand up for others."
– Anonymous

"Never be bullied into silence. Never allow yourself to be made a victim. Accept no one's definition of your life: define yourself."
- Robert Frost

One of the hardest things for a person to do is to be different. We all want to fit in, to be like others, to avoid the threat of ridicule, mocking, or isolation. If we look to the wild, we see a strength in numbers strategy; stay with the herd and a wildebeest is much less likely to be picked off by a hunting lioness; wander off on its own and it sticks out from the others, offering isolation as a tool for the hunter and the promise of easy prey. This

> *"To go against the dominant thinking of your friends, of most of the people you see every day, is perhaps the most difficult act of heroism you can perform."*
>
> - Theodore White, American Journalist

seems to be instinctual in the natural world, and as true for the human psyche as it is for a wild animal's instinct.

Staying with the herd offers protection. From what? Protection from the potential hurt of ridicule for being different. Protection from the potential embarrassment of being wrong, when so many others were right. If one stands with others, even if wrong, there is the security of knowing that the individual is not alone, and therefore free from the threat of the pain of isolation. This fear is powerful, and as such it is the cause of much human suffering. So often, those who know what they are doing is wrong continue to do so because of the safety in numbers philosophy, because of the fear of being different, and conversely, those who want to speak out against the wrong are often quieted by the fear of being ostracized, or worse.

It is not only the fear of being different that so often precludes us from doing the right thing. Martin Niemoller, a prominent protestant pastor during World War II who was a former supporter and then staunch critic of Adolf Hitler's Nazi regime, wrote:

First they came for the Socialists, and I did not speak out—
Because I was not a Socialist.

Then they came for the Trade Unionists, and I did not speak out—
Because I was not a Trade Unionist.

Then they came for the Jews, and I did not speak out—
Because I was not a Jew.

Then they came for me—
and there was no one left to speak for me.

Be A Bean!

When something does not personally affect us, we have a different attitude than if it does. We have a tendency not to worry about things, no matter how wrong, or even evil, if they do not have any impact on our lives or the lives of those we care about. This is the precise reason that evil rises and spreads. This is a major reason that genocides are allowed to scar the very existence of humankind. The holocaust of World War II is a perfect case of good people doing the wrong thing by turning their back on despicable human behavior that just didn't happen to affect them. Non-Jews kept quiet about the atrocities of the Nazis because the Nazis left them alone. The hideous nature of the pure evil was ignored, in large part out of fear of retribution, but also because it didn't affect most of the non-Jewish population. Even the United States of America, the world's greatest force for freedom and human rights in world history, stood by and did nothing to end the Nazi atrocities.

Doing the right thing is not always easy. In fact, there are times when doing the right thing is an enormous personal risk. Being on the "right" side when all others are content to look the other way can leave a person feeling isolated, scrutinized, or even threatened. Being a leader often involves these same feelings – isolation from followers, scrutinized for any and everything that goes wrong, and threatened with the possibility of failure or mutiny. The decision between right and wrong, between making a difference and simply bearing witness, is not always easy. It is not always clear. What a leader must remember is that he or she cannot make a difference without enduring personal risk.

> *"I do not believe in a fate that falls on men however they act; but I do believe in a fate that falls on them unless they act."*
>
> - Buddha

There is always a chance that doing the right thing could lead to the loss of status, loss of respect from certain individuals (although respect from those people should never be a concern), or even loss of friendship (although, one would have to think about how true the friendship was to begin with).

Think about your own lives… how many times have you looked the other way because a wrong did not specifically affect you? Did you ever see someone get bullied and simply turn the other way? Or worse yet, did you ever join in the bullying to be "cool" and ingratiate yourself with the popular kids at the expense of doing the right thing and standing up for those who needed it most? How many times have you turned the other way when you saw someone cheat, or steal, or speak ill of another? Rather than make a difference, you may simply bear witness to wrongdoing, providing safety in your mind, but what about the damage to your heart and soul. What about the damage to others? How will the knowledge of your cowardice of purposely avoiding doing what is right affect you moving forward? What of your self-worth? Could you look in the mirror knowing that the bullying you witnessed, allowed, or participated in, resulted in the suicide of another human being? Knowing that you could have prevented the destruction of another person's life if only you had the courage to stand up against the crowd, to be different, to do what was right in the face of potential adversity… could you really look in the mirror and feel good about who you are?

> *"The most prominent place in hell is reserved for those who are neutral on the great issues of life."*
>
> - Reverend Billy Graham

What is at the heart of the matter when it comes to leadership? ***Leadership is all about making a difference, influencing others to achieve something. This something doesn't happen unless a leader has the strength of character to stand tall when others***

Be A Bean!

shrink...

Do what is right, not what is popular. Always strive to do what you know to be fair and just. Be different when others are striving to be alike. Be bold when others bow. Stand up for those who have no voice, those who have lost hope, or those who simply do not have the strength or courage to stand up for themselves. That is a leader!

Standing by and allowing something wrong to occur when you have the power and ability to stop it is just as bad as committing the wrong by your own actions. A true leader can always look in the mirror and see a man or woman with head held high, a smile of satisfaction, and a heart full of pride looking back... the man or woman in the mirror should always be a person who stands on the side of righteousness and justice.

The question becomes, would you rather struggle through the temporary pains of standing up for what is right or suffer the eternal pain of being on the wrong side of history?

LESSON LEARNED: *Do not be afraid to stand alone, do not fear being different, but rather, always have the courage to be a force for good in this world.*

Keith G. Feit

Be A Bean!

Lesson #3

"Old friends in the day become fresh enemies at night."

Every person has an individual agenda. It is critical for you to understand this, lest you be manipulated to forsake doing what is right for doing what fulfills the selfish needs of others. This is not to say that every individual agenda is in opposition to the greater good, but it is not always easy to distinguish good intentions from selfish ones. Throughout life, others will attempt to influence you in hopes of advancing their own personal agendas. The whispers will be constant. Be your own person. ***Do what you know is right, what you know is just, what you know is best.***

In the early 1960s, as the world sat on the brink of nuclear war, the youngest elected U.S. president in history bore one of the

> *"I prefer to be true to myself, even at the hazard of incurring the ridicule of others, rather than to be false, and incur my own abhorrence."*
>
> - Frederick Douglas

greatest burdens in our nation's history. President John F. Kennedy stood as the man who would determine if there would be a future United States for his children and grandchildren to grow up in, and if that nation would ever again be the "shining city on a hill." The Cuban Missile Crisis became the brink of nuclear holocaust, and the Soviet Union's placement of missiles in Cuba, just 90 miles away from American soil, became the red line in the sand that required the president's immediate attention. As this is not a historical dissertation, we will not delve into the minutiae of the crisis, but rather explore how one man ignored the whispers and listened to the shout of his heart to save the world.

A brief summary of the situation... the Soviet Union refused to remove missiles from sites in Cuba, one of their communist satellite states. This violation of the Monroe Doctrine, in which old world powers were warned to stay out of the Western Hemisphere, could not be allowed to stand, as these missiles posed a serious threat to millions of American lives. Some wanted to appease the Soviets and avoid confrontation, many wanted to strike at the sites and destroy the missiles, and the president was inundated with contradictory advice from the best and brightest this country had to offer. Despite repeated arguments from his leading military advisors counseling for military strikes against the missile sites, actions that could easily provoke retaliation from the Soviet Union and lead to all-out war, Kennedy patiently surveyed the situation seeking the best route to deescalate the situation. His heart told him that engaging in military conflict could lead to devastating outcomes, and in the end, he decided to execute a blockade of Soviet ships delivering missiles and supplies to

> *"In life and love, stay true to yourself. Never change who you are - nor sacrifice what you want – to become what someone else demands."*
>
> - Charles Orlando

Be A Bean!

Cuba. At the red line in the sea, the Russians blinked, turned around, and a back-door agreement was made that allowed the Soviets to save face and remove the missiles. The whispers Kennedy heard could have led to nuclear holocaust, the shout of his heart led the nation off the brink and into calmer, if not peaceful waters.

The lesson from the Cuban Missile Crisis is simple – Be your own person. Listen to advice, but be your own man or woman, make your own decisions based on the best information you have, and live with the consequences knowing that you did what you believed to be best for the greater good. In every aspect of life, do not allow yourself to be manipulated by those with nefarious intentions. Say what you want to say, think what you want to think, do what you want to do, love who you want to love, be what and who you want to be… let your heart guide your life. **Be true to who you are, not to who others expect you to be.** If you follow this path, you will make the right decisions, and you will help leave the world a better place.

> *"Be yourself. Everyone else is already taken."*
> - Oscar Wilde

I have had the good fortune of meeting some of the finest people one could possibly find. One individual, specifically, became someone who I admired greatly. This person had it all – very intelligent, good looks, terrific work ethic, awesome sense of humor, extremely likeable personality… although not perfect, it was a difficult task to find something negative to say. The admiration, however, came not from all these positive traits, but from the heart this individual

> *"The snow goose need not bathe to make itself white. Neither need you do anything but be yourself."*
> - Lao Tzu

displayed for others, and for the strength to stand up and be his own man. He didn't care what the crowd was doing, he was satisfied with who he was, and he did not let others sway him to be something he wasn't. Then the whispers came. Personal jealousies led supposed friends to attempt to manipulate this man to destroy some of the best relationships he had and to deviate from the path of hard work and commitment toward a path of immature actions and professional neglect. The more and more he heard whispers in his ear, the more he changed. He was no longer his own man and the person he truly was, but rather, he became who others wanted or expected him to be. He obviously still had his good looks and intelligence, but the outstanding work ethic that led him to overachieve began to slip. The sense of humor that always put a smile on my face began to disappear. In fact, we barely communicated at all. In a short period of time, the person I admired most in the world had become someone I didn't recognize, and what's worse, although he didn't realize it, he was losing his true identity. Continuing down this path, quelling the shout of his heart in favor of the whispers in his ear, this amazing individual was moving toward a life in which he would settle, for participating in activities others prefer and for a relationship with a person to appease others and make him feel like he is accepted, rather than a person he truly loved. He would begin to act and speak in ways that made him feel worthier to those who mattered little in his life and neglect and ostracize those who were his true rocks. He would become someone that the "man in the glass" couldn't recognize. This is how people lose their way and find not happiness, but regret. Can an individual who is so afraid to be himself or herself be truly happy in life? It is true that you can fool the world into believing something that is not true, but can you

Be A Bean!

fool the man or woman in the glass that looks back at you every day? Eventually, the burden of hiding your true self from the world will lead to excruciating agony, and worse than the damage it will do to you, think of the damage to those you are supposed to love? The husband or wife that eventually finds out the relationship was not based on love; The son or daughter that finds out that the mother or father he or she has looked up to an entire lifetime has been a fraud; The best friend that finds out the he or she could not be trusted to know the truth about who or what his or her closest friend was. For a while, you can fool yourself into believing the façade is real, that the mask is a mere presentation of the true self, but deep down you will always know the truth, and the deeper you bury it, the more wrath you will feel when the day comes for your true self to set itself free.

> *"A man is his own easiest dupe, for what he wishes to be true he generally believes to be true."*
>
> - Demosthenes

If you are afraid to show others who you truly are, then you refuse to admit who you truly are, and if you refuse to admit who you truly are, then you can never become the person you are truly supposed to become. The fulfillment of your destiny rests in your ability to be true to who you are. Listen to others' advice, but do not cower to pressure from external agents. Negotiate with others, be willing to concede on issues that do not derail goal accomplishment, but never compromise on your principle, and never allow others to change who you are or what you stand for. As Thomas Jefferson once said, "In matters of style, swim with the current; in matters of principle, stand like a rock."

Remove the facades, take off the masks, and chase happiness by showing the world the person you see looking back at you in the mirror every day. You can fool others, but you cannot fool the man, or woman, in the glass. He or she who looks back at you from the mirror will look back either with pride or disappointment. Each leads to a different destiny.

> **LESSON LEARNED:** *Listen to the shout of your heart, not the whispers in your ears.*

Be A Bean!

Lesson #4
IT TAKES A TEAM ...

"I long to accomplish a great and noble task, but it is my chief duty to accomplish humble tasks as though they were great and noble. The world is moved along not only by the mighty shoves of its heroes but also by the aggregate of the tiny pushes of each honest worker."
- Helen Keller

How many great leaders have accomplished greatness by their actions alone? Did Alexander the Great conquer the known world without the skilled fighting of his troops? Did George Lucas build his Star Wars empire (no pun intended) without the skills and talents of the various actors, make-up artists, and others who contributed to the film franchise's success? Do American presidents wage war, secure peace, and protect the lives of Americans without a vast cabinet and cadre of military and civilian advisors? Understand that every great feat is accomplished not by the sole actions of an extraordinary person, but by a culmination of the efforts of many.

Isaac Newton is famously quoted as saying, "If I have seen further than others, it is because I have stood on the shoulders of giants." We all stand on the shoulders of others. ***Greatness is not a*** *solitary act but a continuous series of actions that lead to superior results, and no individual in isolation can do it alone.* Individuals might receive the glory, but new heights are never reached in seclusion.

Anyone who knows me, knows I am a big fan of food, especially Italian food. Anyone who has ever made spaghetti knows that it is extremely difficult, if even possible, to take all the hard spaghetti out of the box and break it in half to place it in the pot of boiling water. One must take small bunches of spaghetti at a time. This is like thinking of the individual versus the team. Alone, an individual has many vulnerabilities, weaknesses, and deficiencies. However, add this individual of limited skills and knowledge to a team, and this person becomes much more effective. This individual can rely on the strengths of his or her teammates to limit or negate the impact of the deficiencies or weaknesses the he or she brought to the team. The team is much stronger than the individual, much like the pound of spaghetti together is much stronger than the individual piece of spaghetti.

> *"A great city is that which has the greatest men and women. If it be a few ragged huts, it is still the greatest city in the world."*
>
> - Walt Whitman

There is a reason the president of the United States relies on a cadre of advisors before making decisions. He has an entire cabinet of experts advising him (or one day her) on every aspect of governmental affairs. Why? The team has much more knowledge in more areas than one individual could possibly have. Along with this, the president needs trusted leaders

> *"No leader can be too far ahead of his followers."*
>
> - Eleanor Roosevelt, Former First Lady of USA

Be A Bean!

who can make decisions in his name, such as the Secretary of State making diplomatic decisions or the Secretary of Defense making military decisions (short of war). It would not be efficient, effective, or even possible for the president, any president, to be involved in every bit of minutiae involved in running a bureaucracy as massive as the U.S. government. The president needs a team. The most successful presidents are usually those who have surrounded themselves not with friends and loyalists alone, but those who have dared to surround themselves with the most qualified candidates, including those that often disagree with the president. The greatest example of this is Abraham Lincoln's "Team of Rivals."

As he assumed the presidency of the United States in 1861, Lincoln created a cabinet that a lesser man could never have imagined enduring. First, he chose men who were more experienced in political affairs and much more greatly respected than he. This was a collection of individuals that easily could have outshone the president, and a man of less self-confidence and self-assuredness would cower at the thought of such an arrangement. Secondly, he selected political rivals, such as William Seward, to sit on extremely important cabinet posts, such as Secretary of State. Finally, he appointed Democrats, members of the opposition party, to serve in important positions, including Gideon Welles as Secretary of the Navy and Edwin Stanton as Secretary of War. This team offered the possibility of friction between the highest levels of the cabinet, such as Secretary of State, Secretary of Defense, and the President, at the very least, and governmental dysfunction at worst. However, it also created

> *"Teamwork requires some sacrifice up front; people who work as a team have to put the collective needs of the group ahead of their individual interests.*
>
> - Patrick Lencioni, Leadership Author

an opportunity for diverse viewpoints leading to the development of more creative ideas for dealing with America's issues. Lincoln's ability to utilize the talents of others, weld the differing opinions into wise decisions, and conduct himself as a leader of peers enabled him to earn the respect of even his most ardent former-adversaries. Lincoln needed the experience, knowledge, and expertise of these rivals, and although there was never a question of who was captaining the ship, he was not afraid to rely on the skills and talents of others. At times, he stood on the shoulders of rivals to ensure the continued survival and success of the union, guiding it through the darkest time in our nation's history, the Civil War.

Reality is that very few leaders have the self-assurance to lead in such a manner with the threat of surrounding themselves with more capable and respected individuals. In my professional career, there has only been one administrator who has been confident enough in her own abilities to do this. The leaders I have worked for have generally been insecure, surrounding themselves with yes men, fearing those who demonstrate ability and dare to disagree or have an opinion in opposition to that of the leadership. This is the worst kind of leadership – it tends to reward incompetence and punish initiative; it promotes groupthink and resists individuality. Organizations with this type of leadership typically see the loss of productive members in favor of less competent individuals, as those with less skill, less ambition, and less independence present a lesser threat than those who challenge the status quo. Don't be this kind of leader. Be a leader who surrounds himself or herself with independent thinking, highly competent individuals with diverse skills and views.

> LESSON LEARNED: *Never let pride get in your way of seeking and accepting help, and never let ego lead to diminishing the importance of the efforts of others in all your successes.*

Be A Bean!

Lesson #5
CHASE PERFECTION, ACHIEVE EXCELLENCE

"Perfection is not attainable, but if we chase perfection we can catch excellence."

- Vince Lombardi

Michael J. Fox once said that he is careful not to confuse excellence with perfection, because while he can attempt to achieve excellence, only God can deal with perfection. No doubt it is true perfection is impossible to reach, but it should never be impossible to strive for. As Vince Lombardi said, chasing perfection is a path to achieving excellence.

> *"We are what we repeatedly do. Excellence, then, is not an act but a habit."*
>
> - Confucius

What loftier goal than perfection? Impossible to reach, but not impossible to aspire to. Impossible to find, but not impossible to inspire. While we all know that it is impossible for any man or woman to achieve perfection, if that is where we have set our sights, how can we not succeed? ***It might not be possible to play the perfect game, write the perfect essay, or give the perfect speech, but it is possible to give perfect effort, to have perfect commitment and dedication, and to move forward with perfect preparation.*** The goal of perfection may be unattainable, but the ability to act in ways that bring perfection closer to reality are not only possible, but readily available.

Don't get me wrong... I am not saying it is easy to put in the amount of hard work, to display the persistence, to adopt the attitude, and to fulfill the commitment and dedication required to chase perfection and achieve excellence. I am saying it is easy to figure out what it takes. It is easy to determine the steps needed to reach the loftiest of goals. However, that is where easy ends and difficult begins. How many people are willing to go through the grind, to sacrifice the time and energy, to be the best? Blood, sweat, tears, pain, sorrow, adversity... these are not the enemy, not things we should shy away from. They are the landmarks that we can use to find our way to the "Promised land." These are the stamps of approval that seal an individual's march to extraordinary. These are the hallmarks of success. These are the signs of an individual chasing perfection. These are the requirements of achieving excellence.

> *"Excellence is the gradual result of always striving to do better."*
>
> - Pat Riley

I remember watching the Disney classic, *Remember the Titans*, with my basketball team back in the early 2000s. We were watching to be inspired by the adversity T.C. Williams high was forced to endure and overcome on their way to a championship season. Coach Herman Boone, at least as portrayed by Denzel Washington in the movie, demanded perfection from his players,

Be A Bean!

> *"You will be perfect in every aspect of the game. You drop a pass, you run a mile. You miss a blocking assignment, you run a mile. You fumble the football, and I will break my foot off in your John Brown hind parts and then you will run a mile. Perfection. Let's go to work."*

I believe in demanding perfection from my players, as well. I believe a leader's responsibility is to demand perfection from all followers. As we mentioned earlier, perfection is not possible, but the pursuit of perfection is. It may not be possible to play a perfect basketball game, but this should not inhibit an individual's ability or desire to put forth perfect effort, to go forth with perfect preparation, and to play with a desire to play the perfect game. Should the difficulty of scoring a 100% on an exam lead a student to give less than perfect effort in taking notes, understanding reading assignments, and studying for the exam? Should the slim chance of a raise or promotion lead an employee to perform his or her job assignments with any less desire to achieve perfection in the outcome of such tasks?

The United States of America has the greatest armed forces in the history of the world. The soldiers, sailors, pilots, marines, and every member of the services undergo rigorous training to ensure that each and every individual is capable of performing in the field of battle. This training is aimed at pursuing perfection in every aspect of war. Is perfection pursued to ensure that every soldier is the perfect soldier, or every pilot operates with the precision of a computer? Of course not. However, by pursuing perfection in training, the U.S Armed Forces are guaranteeing the excellence of the nation's fighting forces.

The pursuit of perfection is not about attaining perfection, but about achieving excellence. **Pursuing perfection allows individuals, teams, organizations, and even nations, to ensure their best chance at realizing potential, achieving goals, and** *creating future opportunities.*

> **LESSON LEARNED:** *Although perfection is unattainable, we must strive to reach perfection if we are to achieve excellence.*

Lesson #6
SPEAK TO HOPE, NOT FEAR

> "May your choices reflect your hopes, not your fears."
> – Nelson Mandela

"And whatever else history may say about me when I'm gone, I hope it will record that I appealed to your best hopes, not your worst fears, to your confidence rather than your doubts."

- President Ronald Reagan

    The old saying goes, "there is more than one way to skin a cat." That statement is profound, and so true in all aspects of life. If we confine ourselves to a reality where there is only one solution or one correct answer, then we are stifling the creativity born of experimentation and exploration that is required to expand our horizons. Along those lines, there are multiple ways to motivate others to work toward individual and organizational goals. Human beings are motivated by various emotions – fear, anger, love, despair, etc. An effective leader can push the right buttons to reach each individual's "motivator." While some individuals do react well to the fear of failure or punishment, the commitment born out of fear is much less powerful and enduring than a commitment born of positive emotions.

    President Ronald Reagan, the 40th president of the United States, was affectionately known as "The Great Communicator." As a former actor, he played up his performances in front of the

> "Consult not your fears but your hopes and your dreams. Think not about your frustrations, but about your unfulfilled potential. Concern yourself not with what you tried and failed in, but with what it is still possible for you to do.
>
> - Pope John XXIII

cameras and portrayed himself as a cheerleader for the American people, always showing his fellow citizens that he, the eternal optimist, would always be looking forward to better days. Reagan told us that his nickname came not from his skills as an orator, but rather from the fact the he "communicated great things." It was the hopes, aspirations, dreams, and pride of the American people that he spoke to, always reminding us of American exceptionalism, that made him a beloved leader. His ability to speak to our hopes separated him from many average or even above average politicians and public servants, leading him to be regarded as one of America's greatest presidents. While the American spirit was damaged and hurtling in a downward spiral during the "malaise" of the Carter years, Reagan dared to speak not of an America in decline, but of a "shining city on a hill" that was a beacon to all freedom-loving people everywhere. He reminded us that our best days were always ahead of us, and that together, we could "Make America Great Again." While others focused on the problems of the day and spoke to our common fears, Reagan emphasized the opportunity of tomorrow by reminding us of why we were the greatest nation in the history of the world. While for President Carter and other leaders of the day it seemed as though the sun was setting, and night was falling on the United States, for Reagan it was always "Morning in America," as the sun was eternally rising on a better tomorrow. It was this ability to communicate effectively to American's hopes and to lessen their fears of a darker tomorrow that spurred millions to follow the president through what became known as the "Reagan Revolution." This revolution rejuvenated national pride, revitalized an ailing economy, brought down communism, freed millions of people all over the world from totalitarian rule, and left the United States standing as the world's lone superpower. The power of words, the appeal to the emotion of hope, emphasizing dreams rather than nightmares… these were the engines of national renewal.

It is hard to overestimate the importance of appealing to the hopes of your followers, rather than their fears. The motivational power of fear dissipates once failure has been averted, while the motivational influence of hope extends beyond failure, beyond success, to always reaching for something better. As long as we hope for something better, as long as we believe there is something better, something just out of reach, then our internal motivation will continue to drive us to greatness. Fear is an external driver, pushing us to act in an attempt to prevent negative consequences from befalling us. Hope is an internal driver, exhorting us to push as hard as we can to realize our potential. When we allow fear to be our driver, we limit ourselves to merely trying to prevent the actualization of our visions of doom and gloom. When we speak to our followers' hopes, we open their eyes to the potential of a brighter future, and earn their support. Ronald Reagan understood this when, in 1975, he implored the reeling Republican Party, and conservative movement in general, that "Our task is to make [the people] see that what we represent is identical to their own hopes and dreams of what America can and should be."

> *"A leader is a dealer in hope."*
> - Napoleon Bonaparte

It's important to remember that great leaders speak to the hearts of their followers, not their minds. Logical pleas, while effective in certain technical situations, do not engender the same passion, loyalty, and enthusiasm as those of emotional pleas. *When you speak to someone's hopes, you are appealing to their most basic emotions, and taking the most direct route to their heart.*

> LESSON LEARNED: *The most effective way to inspire others is by finding a way into their hearts; the easiest path into an individual's heart is through the realization of his or her hopes and dreams.*

Lesson #7
 CELEBRATE FAILURE

"Failure is simply the opportunity to begin again, this time more intelligently."
- Henry Ford

"Success consists of going from failure to failure with no loss of enthusiasm."
- Sir Winston Churchill

Who in life hasn't failed? The greatest of all leaders have had their moments of doubt, instances of poor decisions, and actions that have led to failure. Winston Churchill once exclaimed, "Success is not permanent, and failure is not fatal." Oprah Winfrey has stated that failure is a stepping stone to success. I believe the path to success can actually be thought of as a staircase, with the ultimate goal at the very top. The staircase, depending on the ultimate outcome desired and the difficulty in achieving such an outcome, can be relatively short or extremely high. The number of steps is dependent on the height of the staircase. Those steps are a combination of wins and losses, victories and defeats, successes and failures... however you wish to describe actions that work and don't work or decisions that prove to be right or wrong. The more difficult the outcome is to

> *"Only those who dare to fail greatly can ever achieve greatly."*
>
> - Robert F. Kennedy,
> U.S. Attorney General and Presidential Candidate

achieve, the more we need to take chances and learn, meaning there is a greater probability of an increased number of failures along the way, hence a taller staircase. Each time we learn from a failure, we succeed in some small way... thus, we have taken another step, advancing further up the staircase and closer to our goal.

Without the foundation built on our failures, we can never reach the ultimate success. It is our failures that teach us what doesn't work and grants us another opportunity to figure out what will work. Scientists speak of trial and error...the trial is the attempt; the error is the failure; it is these errors that eliminate things that don't work so that we can eventually determine what will. On the Staircase of Success (Figure #1), each failure leads to a small success, with failure possible in every action we take or decision we make in the process of attempting to reach our final goal. Each failure represents the opportunity for another win on the road to success, and another step on the staircase... until finally, we reach the ultimate goal.

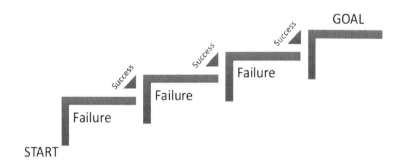

Figure 1. Staircase to Success

What is a failure? According to Thomas Edison, there is no such thing. In his words, he has never failed. He just simply found

Be A Bean!

thousands of ways that didn't work. What an inspiring way to look at failing to meet our own expectations! If you think about failure as nothing more than something that didn't work, you would be more likely to use the failure to learn, to try something new after eliminating what did not work, and to continue to persist without losing faith. Looking at the staircase, one can see that every time we find a way that doesn't work (failure) we find an alternative way that works (success). That's how we climb! If a person persists, he or she will continue to climb the staircase, eventually reaching the desired outcome (goal).

> *"If you're not making mistakes, then you're not doing anything. I'm positive that doers make mistakes."*
>
> - John Wooden,
> Hall of Fame Basketball Coach

As Edison also advises, "Our greatest weakness lies in giving up. The most certain way to succeed is to always try just one more time." If we stop when we reach a setback, we can never climb to the next step. We need our failures to learn; we need our failures to motivate us to find a way that works. If Edison gave up when his original attempts at the light bulb failed, how much longer would humanity have wandered in a world without that electric wonder?

Success follows hard work, smiles often follow tears, triumph often follows failure. Winston Churchill once said, "Success is not final, failure is not fatal; it is the courage to continue that counts." He also defined success as "the ability to go from one failure to another with no loss of enthusiasm." Those who are victorious in life are those who can use failure as motivation to work harder and find a way to overcome. Just listen to Churchill... failure is not fatal; it is not the end unless we allow it to prevent us from continuing to move forward. I dare to go a step further than Churchill, by telling you today that not only is failure not fatal, it is necessary. As Oprah Winfrey once said, every failure is a stepping stone to eventual success. We learn from our failure; we grow from our failures. I challenge you to not only accept failure as a part of life, but to celebrate failure as the engine of success. Failure may not seem to fit in the pursuit of perfection, but failing as you chase perfection is integral to achieving excellence.

Take Steve Jobs, for example, The Apple icon who is most famous for the creation of the iPod, Ipad, and iPhone, who revolutionized technology and gave rise to the era of smart technology. Jobs was faced with many failures that could have ended his pursuit of technological advances. His new business venture, after being removed as CEO of Apple, NeXT computer, was a miserable failure. The Apple III, Powermac g4 cube, and Apple Lisa were among the products that failed. However, he learned from these failures and embraced these setbacks as learning experiences. Despite these failures, or more likely because of them, Jobs went on to be one of the most celebrated business leaders and technology visionaries of all-time. Jobs' ability to overcome failure impacted the world technologically. Others have a profound impact on our society, and even civilization, socially, economically, politically, etc.

> *"Success is not final, failure is not fatal; it is the courage to continue that counts."*
>
> - Sir Winston Churchill, Prime Minister of Great Britain during World War II

Winston Churchill, arguably the greatest war-time civilian leader in world history, suffered many setbacks before finally marching into the history books as the savior of western civilization following World War II. He was born with a lisp, yet went on to be one of the greatest orators of the English language ever to grace the international scene. Despite failures as a student, he went on to be one of the most respected leaders on the world stage and a legendary figure in the lore of English-speaking

Be A Bean!

people. After being removed as First Lord of the Admiralty for Great Britain in 1915 following his decision to support the disastrous Gallipoli campaign in World War I, losing numerous elections, and many years in "the wilderness," Churchill assumed the post of Prime Minister of Great Britain in 1940. This was the darkest time in the nation's history; all its allies had fallen or were about to fall to Hitler's Nazi Germany, the United States remained a bystander, and the British stood alone against the Axis juggernaut. All he did then, with Western civilization hanging in the balance, was lead the British and the allies to victory over the most evil force the world had ever seen, against what seemed to be insurmountable odds. As others searched for ways to sugarcoat each defeat, Churchill boldly pronounced failure as loudly as he did victory, constantly rallying the British people to the cause. Each failure along the lengthy and storied career of Winston Churchill made him the leader he would become during World War II, refusing to succumb to the circumstances of the day. If not for the learning that occurred with every failure, if not for Churchill's ability to go from "failure to failure with no loss of enthusiasm," the world could very well be a different looking place than it is today, and not for the better.

If we live by the words, thoughts, and actions of Winston Churchill and Thomas Edison, then we lead by embracing failure as a necessity, and much less as the closing of the only door to success, but rather as the opening of new, previously unknown doors. Remember, closing the door to one path usually opens the door to many more.

> **LESSON LEARNED:** *Failure is not the end, but a new beginning; it is an opportunity to learn, to grow, and to find a new path to success.*

Keith G. Feit

Lesson #8
BE THE MASTER OF YOUR FATE

"Men are not prisoners of fate, but only prisoners of their own minds."
- Franklin D. Roosevelt

"Destiny is no matter of chance. It is a matter of choice. It is not a thing to be waited for, it is a thing to be achieved."
-William Jennings Bryan

You determine the ceiling on your achievements. You decide how high you can go. The goals you set for yourself and the standards by which you live will determine the ceiling set for your success. The real questions are how high do you want to go? What do you want to achieve? Do you want to stand out? Do you want to be the best? Do you want to blaze your own trail or settle for following the pack?

When I came across the poem, *Invictus*, written by William Earnest Henley in the late 1800s, it spoke to me about the essence of leadership and the key to living a happy and productive life. Neuroscience research in

> *"It is not in the stars to hold our destiny but in ourselves."*
>
> - William Shakespeare

leadership has determined there are two types of people in terms of how we look at who or what controls the outcomes in our lives. People with an internal locus of control believe that the individual him or herself is in control of what happens in life. In contrast, those with an external locus of control believe that luck, chance, powerful external agents, or some other factor out of the control of the individual is responsible for life's outcomes. In *Invictus*, Henley is telling us that it is you who controls your destiny, you and you alone, regardless of the adversity faced over the course of a lifetime.

If you heed his words and take them to heart, live by the thoughts contained in this poem, then you have an internal locus of control. With the belief that you control the outcomes in your life based on the decisions you make and the actions you take, you will be happier, you will have more hope, and you will achieve greater success. As a leader with such a locus of control, you will offer more hope to your followers that they, too, can control their own fate and be masters of their own destinies. With such a belief, they will be more motivated to put forth great effort knowing that the outcomes they experience, either positive or negative, will be determined by the strength of those efforts.

It is your challenge to have an "unconquerable soul" when faced with adversity, to be "unbowed" when you are down and taking tough hits, and to be "unafraid" of future challenges and the veil of darkness that lurks with every potential failure. As the captain of your fate, you must have the strength to captain your soul through even the roughest waters.

> *"Control your own destiny or someone else will."*
>
> \- Jack Welch

It is easy for us, as humans, to search for excuses or to cast blame for negative outcomes in hopes of saving ourselves the embarrassment of admitting the failure was our own. However, what positive comes from finding an excuse or laying blame?

While the temporary avoidance of admitting weakness or areas of personal deficit may promote an initial feeling of victory, that elation will wear off quickly as the disappointments of future failures add up due to lack of acknowledgement of deficiencies and growth in those areas.

Your effort, and the effort of those who follow you, will be determined in large part by the realization that we determine the circumstances of our lives by the words we speak, the decisions we make, and the actions we take.

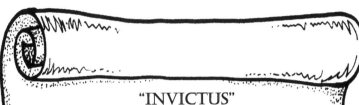

"INVICTUS"

Out of the night that covers me,
Black as the pit from pole to pole,
I thank whatever gods may be
For my unconquerable soul.

In the fell clutch of circumstance
I have not winced nor cried aloud.
Under the bludgeonings of chance
My head is bloody, but unbowed.

Beyond this place of wrath and tears
Looms but the Horror of the shade,
And yet the menace of the years
Finds, and shall find me, unafraid.

It matters not how strait the gate,
How charged with punishments the scroll,
I am the master of my fate:
I am the captain of my soul.

- William Ernest Henley (c. 1888)

Be A Bean!

The parable below, telling the story of an ancient general, presents the power of locus of control. Who controls your destiny; who determines your fate? Read the parable and understand its message.

> *"Once upon a time, there was a general who was leading his army into battle against an enemy with an army ten times the size of his own.*
>
> *Along the way to the battle field, the troops stopped by a small temple to pray for victory. The general held up a coin and told his troops, "I am going to implore the gods to help us crush our enemy. If this coin lands with the heads on top, we'll win. If it's tails, we'll lose. Our fate is in the hands of the gods. Let us pray wholeheartedly."*
>
> *After a short prayer, the general tossed the coin. It landed with heads on top.*
>
> *The troops were overjoyed and went into the battle with high spirit. The smaller army, believing the Gods were on their side, won the battle. The soldiers were exalted, "It's good to have the gods on our side! No one can change what they have determined."*
>
> *"Really?" asked the General, showing them the coin -- both sides of it were heads."*

What does this parable teach us? It will not be your parents, teachers, coaches, bosses, spouses, or friends that will determine what you accomplish in life. In the end, there is only one person who will determine how successful you will be, and that person looks back at you in the mirror every day. A true

> *"It is in the moments of decision that your destiny is shaped."*
>
> - Tony Robbins

leader understands this, and works not to satisfy the desires of all those that follow, but rather the desires of the man or woman in the glass, for the desires of a true leader will fulfill the needs of both individual followers and the organization, as a whole. If a leader is driven by ethical decisions, then the greater good will always outweigh individual ambitions. Success is determined by the combined efforts of many, not an individual person, but it is the decisions of the leader that sets the tone and fosters the culture and climate within the organization that ultimately leads to victory or defeat. In the end, you, by your decisions, actions, attitudes, interactions, and relationships, will determine if your coin is heads on both sides.

> LESSON LEARNED: *There can only be one captain guiding a ship, and you are the captain of your ship. The journey is yours to travel and the destination is yours to decide. You are the master of your fate.*

Be A Bean!

"We do not admire a man of timid peace."
- Theodore Roosevelt

Lesson #9
PAINT IN BOLD COLORS, NOT PALE PASTELS

"Far better is it to dare mighty things, to win glorious triumphs, even though checkered by failure, than to take rank with those poor spirits who neither enjoy much nor suffer much, because they live in the gray twilight that knows not victory nor defeat."
- President Theodore Roosevelt

A Latin proverb states, "Fortune favors the bold, but abandons the timid." It needs no explanation. To go further, not only does fortune look down upon the bold, but the bold, in fact, make their own good fortune. When Steve Jobs hired John Sculley of Pepsi as CEO of Apple, it took quite a sales job for the 29-year old visionary to lure a successful leader of a major international corporation. He did so by painting a picture of bold colors, asking Sculley, "Do you want to sell sugar water for the rest of your life, or do you want to come with me and change the world?"

Steve jobs was a visionary who never painted his visions of the future in pale pastels; he was always bold and always looking not just to lead the market, but to create new markets. He dared to risk, and because of his bold approach to innovation, we are now in an age of smart technology, from smart phones to touch screen tablets, to smart watches, and probably some things of which I am not even aware. Many would say he not only created new markets, but created a new world.

In a 1975 speech, then-former California governor and future president Ronald Reagan challenged the Republican Party to stand for something, in stark contrast to the Democrat party, and to proudly clarify the distinctions,

> *"Our people look for a cause to believe in. Is it a third party we need, or is it a new and revitalized second party, raising a banner of no pale pastels, but bold colors which make it unmistakably clear where we stand on all of the issues troubling the people?"*

Reagan was making it clear that the Republican Party could not go on continuing to paint in pale pastels. In other words, if the Republicans were so afraid to campaign on their differences with the Democrats, then disaffected members of the party would seek to establish a third party, one that would boldly and proudly stand for the issues important to them. After a "pale pastels" campaign of Gerald Ford ended with Democrats taking the White House in 1976, Reagan painted in bold colors in the election of 1980, winning in a landslide and ushering in the "Reagan Revolution" that fundamentally influenced the nation's political and economic systems, and international standing for decades to come.

> *"Better to fight for something than live for nothing."*
>
> - General George Patton

General George Patton, one of the leading American military commanders in World War II, never one to shy away from controversy or back away from making his beliefs painfully clear to the world, and one of the most successful military leaders in history, once announced, "Nobody ever defended anything successfully, there is only attack and attack, and attack some more." Much like Reagan implored conservatives to go on the offensive against the liberal ideology, Patton suggested that we should always be on the offensive. An old adage in sports says that

Be A Bean!

the best defense is a good offense. Playing defense is painting with pale pastels, going on the attack is painting in bold colors.

As a leader, painting in bold colors means more than just taking aggressive or risky action. That is certainly part of it, but being bold means not being afraid to be different. If you want people to follow you, it is not good enough just to say you are a good leader or a good person. I would ask that person, why are you better than someone else? When I vote for a representative, or governor, or president, I don't just want to hear the talking points of conservatism or liberalism that every candidate memorizes and spews in order to win votes; I want to know why one candidate is better for my future and the future of my country than the other candidates – What are the differences between them? I don't want a candidate who is afraid to offend voters, so they tell us what they think we want to hear and try not to deviate from conventional wisdom and popular demand. I want to vote for a leader, and a leader is one who proudly pronounces his or her differences on positions, proudly promotes his or her innovative, and potentially risky ideas, and proudly tells the voters not why he or she is the "safe" choice, but why he or she is the "Right" choice. If you like playing it safe, accept a role as a follower. If you want to lead, safe needs to be replaced with bold. There is no safety in leadership!

The American Revolution saw American rebels suffering defeat after defeat in the early stages of the war. After losing New York and being forced to retreat to Pennsylvania, General George Washington, Commander-in-Chief of the patriots' Continental Army, was desperate for a much-needed win to improve morale, stem the tide of soldiers deserting the independence effort, and prevent the Continental Congress from losing faith in the chances for victory. On December 25, 1776, Washington made the bold decision to cross the icy Delaware River into Trenton, New Jersey, and

> *"We may make mistakes – but they must never be mistakes which result from faintness of heart or abandonment of moral principle."*
>
> - Franklin Delano Roosevelt, U.S. President

commence a sneak attack on the Hessian mercenaries hired by the British to fight the Americans. This crossing included not only his troops, but also the cannons of General Henry Knox. To cross a river in such conditions was difficult enough, but to do so with such discipline as to avoid any alerting of the enemy was a tremendous feat. Washington's strategy involved a three-pronged approach, but unfortunately, the other two armies Washington expected could not engage in the assault. Washington, however, understood the importance of this mission, and continued with his bold plans. After dividing his men, he sent flanking columns on opposite sides to outflank the Hessians. The surprise attack succeeded, with 104 casualties and 918 prisoners taken. Only 400 Hessians escaped the American rout.

Knowing he could not stand up to General Cornwallis' army that currently had the Continentals pinned down, Washington again decided to be both bold and sneaky. While the British slept, Washington ordered a few hundred men to stay behind and keep the campfires going while the rest of his army began a night march to Princeton. As Cornwallis and his officers were tricked into thinking the Americans remained camped near Trenton, Washington led his troops to a victory over a regular British army in the field at Princeton. Washington's bold leadership improved morale and proved to the soldiers, the Continental Congress, and all those who believed in the patriots' cause that the commander-in-chief could effectively lead the Continental Army to victory.

Painting in bold colors does not only mean taking risk and being different. It also means being willing to make enemies. Winston Churchill once said, "You have enemies. Good, that means you have stood for something at some point in your life." A leader cannot be afraid to offend, any more than they can be afraid to be different or take chances. If you didn't already know it, a leader must do what is right, not what is popular. These two are often diametrically opposed, meaning that by doing the right thing, a leader is going to offend a

> *"Think little goals and expect little achievements. Think big goals and win big success."*
>
> - Joseph David Schwartz, American Businessman

good number of people. ***If you want to be everyone's friend, be a follower***. It is impossible to make everyone happy with every decision, or benefit every person with every action. That is not a leader's job. A leader's job is to have a positive impact on the greatest number of people, to make decisions and take actions in a way that promotes success within the organization, and behave in a way that fosters a culture that breeds such success. To accomplish this, a leader must be able to provide an achievable and desirable vision of the future, and then ensure the followers have a path to make that vision a reality by providing direction and gaining buy-in so all followers march in that direction.

I firmly believe in being bold, in thinking and acting differently. It has never bothered me to stand alone on an island, even if the rest of the world were against me, if I knew what I was doing was what was right or what was best. This philosophy is best summed up in a passage from www.wisdomcommons.org, which states:

> *"Boldness is being willing to take risks in the service of what matters. It means being courageous, speaking or acting in the face of possible danger or rebuke. Boldness doesn't mean lacking fear or anxiety, rather it means pushing past these to do what is right –*
> *or what makes your heart sing.*
>
> *Boldness helps us to translate our values into tangible action. When we are bold, we are willing to risk shame and etiquette for what is right. We dare to publicly fail if need be, and our willingness to risk failure leads at times to exhilarating successes. Clarity about our purpose and passions makes us bold."*

I also believe strongly in creativity. Leaders must be willing to creatively disrupt the internal and external environments to achieve progress, and they must be willing to take chances on creative solutions to problems if the organization is to survive and thrive in the constantly changing markets of our current postmodern condition.

Being creative is painting in bold colors; challenging conventional wisdom is painting in bold colors; taking chances and being different is painting in bold colors; standing up for what is right, regardless of risk is painting in bold colors… ***pale pastels should only be used on a canvas of mediocrity; bold colors are the path to a masterpiece of excellence, progress, and a bright new future.***

> ***LESSON LEARNED:*** *The boldness of our actions will determine the distance we travel. The timid are bound by the limitations of their fear; the bold are unleashed to soar to new heights.*

Lesson #10
SHAVE THE DARN BIRD!

"If the rate of change on the outside exceeds the rate of change on the inside, the end is near"
- Jack Welch

"I hold it that a little rebellion now and then is a good thing, and as necessary in the political world as storms in the physical"
- Thomas Jefferson

It is said that one plucks a bird one feather at a time. I say, why wait? Shave the darn bird! This philosophy deals specifically with how we approach the status quo. In other words, how do we deal with change – Do we embrace change or fear it? Do we mange change or lead it? These are critical questions that we need to answer if we expect to make progress. As John Kotter suggests in his seminal work, *Leading Change*, "Management makes a system work. It helps you do what you know how to do. Leadership builds systems or transforms old ones." Plucking feathers is managing, shaving the bird is leading. You need to decide if you simply want to keep the current system functioning efficiently or if you want to transform the system and create something great. Are you a plucker or a shaver?

Maintaining the status quo is keeping things stable, ensuring today will be just as good as yesterday, and tomorrow will be just as good as today. The problem is, with the status quo, chances are that tomorrow will not be better than today. A true leader should never be satisfied with the status quo, even in good times. ***It can never be true that things cannot get better, for that would mean we have reached perfection.*** As we all know, perfection is an impossible destination to reach, but a beautiful port for which to sail. We should never allow our ship to stay docked at the status quo, for if we do we will never experience the beauty on the horizon just ahead.

In his acceptance speech at the Democratic National Convention in 1960, John F. Kennedy, the future president dared America to be great, to never settle for ordinary but to always strive for extraordinary. He spoke to the spirit of American exceptionalism, asserting the firm belief that the status quo is not good enough, should never be considered good enough, and that we can always reach higher, travel further, and achieve greater. Heed these words from the 35th President of the United States, speaking of the unsolved problems and unanswered questions of the day in what he called the New Frontier:

> *"...a choice that lies... between national greatness and national decline – between the fresh air of progress and the stale, dank atmosphere of 'normalcy' – between determined dedication and creeping mediocrity."*

Shaving the bird means going for the gold, not holding anything back. The pluckers are those people who are so afraid of change that any effort to implement change is so incremental and minimal that it barely registers as a deviation from the status quo. The shavers are those individuals bold enough to go where no man (or woman) has gone before. These are the individuals who break barriers, find new cures, create new technologies, and generally improve lives.

Be A Bean!

Massive change is not always required and sometimes pluckers could be charting the right course, but when change is needed, do not torture the bird by slowly plucking it one feather at a time...put it out of its misery quickly - boldly disrupt the status quo with transformational change. Just as a bird suffers with a slow defeathering, your organization could suffer with the stagnancy caused by slow, fearful efforts to implement incremental change when the competition is revolutionizing the market with a "shave the bird" mentality. In Lesson #11, we talk about changing the rules of the game, or even changing the game, itself. Incremental changers, those pluckers, are generally those who play by the rules with a resulting lack of progress. True progress is made by those who, like Thomas Edison, ignore the rules, or those like Richard Branson, who change the rules. These are transformational figures who altered markets, lives, and society. These are individuals who weren't afraid to shave the darn bird!

> *"It is not the strongest of the species that survives, nor the most intelligent that survives. It is the one that is most adaptable to change."*
>
> - Charles Darwin

LESSON LEARNED: *Timid pursuits of change lead to stagnancy, while aggressive pursuits lead to progress. Incremental change and efforts to manage the status quo can lead to organizational success, but it is transformational change and those who enthusiastically lead such movements that change the world.*

Keith G. Feit

Be A Bean!

Lesson #11
CHANGE THE RULES

"You either play by the rules, change the rules, or get out, altogether."
Michael Eisner, CEO of The Disney Co.

Thomas Edison professed that there are no rules if you want to accomplish something. Richard Branson concurred, crediting breaking rules with producing the change required for progress. Both make excellent points regarding the limitations of rules.

Rules often get in the way of the growth and development of individuals and organizations, erecting barriers to action, risk, creativity, and innovation. Rules often separate ordinary from extraordinary – those tied to the rules can be bound to ordinary results while those who risk the consequences of broken rules frequently unleash the power of human ingenuity, resulting in extraordinary accomplishments. The other side of the

> *"If everybody followed the rules, there would be no change. Without change, there would be no progress."*
>
> - Richard Branson, Founder of Virgin Atlantic

coin, however, is not all roses and rainbows. Rules are often necessary and play an important role in establishing order and providing organizations with the guidelines that allow a variety of individuals to accomplish diverse tasks. In the end, rules, in and of themselves, are not the enemy of success, excellence, or progress. Some rules should be followed while others should be broken. Many can, and should, be eliminated. It is not, however, the existence of rules that hinder excellence, it's not knowing how to use the rules to one's advantage that halts the journey to extraordinary.

Leadership is not about following the rules. It's also not about breaking the rules. Leadership is about making the rules!

The question is… Do you control the rules or do the rules control you? An effective leader influences followers. A leader who excels influences not only his or her followers, his or her organization, and his or her community… an excellent leader influences the market, the environment, and even society, in general. Why play by someone else's rules? Why play a game that aids the competition and puts your organization at a disadvantage? That's not what William Jefferson Clinton did in 1992, when he was elected President of the United States.

Election after election, the Democrats put up liberals to campaign for the presidency. In 1984, it was former Vice President, Walter Mondale, who went on to lose the electoral vote to President Ronald Reagan 525-13 in the largest landslide in U.S. presidential election history. He only won his home state of Minnesota and Washington D.C., also losing the popular vote by nearly 18 million! In 1988, it didn't get much better, as former Massachusetts governor Michael Dukakis lost to Vice President George H.W. Bush 426-111 with nearly 7 million

> *"Hell, there are no rules. We are trying to accomplish something."*
>
> - Thomas Edison

Be A Bean!

less votes. The liberal-conservative game wasn't working for the Democrats, so in 1992, Bill Clinton changed the rules of the game. He did not campaign as a liberal, but rather as what he called a "New Democrat," a more moderate Democrat who was not proudly espousing liberal policies like increased taxes and support of the welfare state. Clinton refused to play a game in which the rules were rigged against him, so he not only altered the rules, but changed the game entirely. He went on to defeat incumbent President George H.W. Bush by approximately 5 million votes, and a 370-168 advantage in the electoral college.

When the rules of the game don't work for you or your organization, change the rules. In fact, change the game completely, so that your competition is forced to play by your rules. Never allow your competition to gain home-field advantage. Make them play on your turf, by your rules, where you are more comfortable.

We all know the parable of the tortoise and the hare, where the slow and steady tortoise beats the much faster, yet overconfident hare in a race. If the hare had run consistently as hard as he could have, he easily would have won the race. Let's say he did that... how could the tortoise possibly win in a race against the hare? He could change the rules of the race:

> *The tortoise realized that there's no way he can beat the hare in a normal race. He thought for a while, and after formulating his strategy, he challenged the hare to a race on a specific course upon which he decided. The hare agreed.*
>
> *They started off. The hare took off and ran at top speed, easily leading the tortoise, until he came to a broad river. The finishing line was just on the other side of the river.*

The hare sat there trying to figure out how to get across the river. Meanwhile, the tortoise labored along, got into the river, swam to the other side, and continued walking until he finished the race.

The tortoise had beaten the hare, even when the hare ran his fastest from start to finish.

The tortoise could not compete on a straight course, as the hare was much faster. However, incapable of swimming, that hare was disadvantaged by the tortoise designing a course with a start and end line separated by water. Despite being much slower and incapable of winning a race on the original course, the tortoise changed the trajectory of the race by changing the course. He forced the hare to race on his turf, and in this situation, it was the hare who could not compete.

As Director of Athletics of a combination school (K-12), I was responsible for building a program at a school that emphasized academics and S.T.E.M. programs. Sports were not even on the list of priorities, even at the lowest level. When I first took the job, there was an administration that always made decisions based on what was best for the students. The support for what we were trying to do in the athletic department was tremendous, and we began to build something special. One of our issues with the high school was that the students were fully dual-enrolled in college courses for their high school credit, limiting the ability of students to participate in interscholastic athletics. This caused many missed practices, missed games, and very little off-season development opportunities. We could not possibly compete with the traditional schools in our district – they weren't like us. Even though we had enough students to be in a

> *"Rules are made for people who aren't willing to make up their own."*
>
> - Chuck Yeager

Be A Bean!

higher classification, this was not an accurate representation of our ability to field competitive teams because most students could not participate. I decided to change the rules of the game. We were going to compete on a much more level playing field.

The state sanctioning body separates teams into classifications, regions, and districts based on school population and geography. As mentioned earlier, due to our special circumstances as a research lab school, we struggled to even compete in this system. Through much communication, persuasion, and persistence, I was able to work with a few other athletic directors/coaches to form a boys' basketball conference. We still maintained our membership in the state and competed in the state district, but we opened up a new opportunity for our students. The conference started with 6 teams of similar situations. The conference expanded to 8 teams and we added a championship tournament at the end of the season. After four years, our school had won two conference championships, our players were proud, our fans were excited, and we finally had a growing sports program. Other schools also saw an increase in team pride and school spirit.

If you can't compete with the other team's size, make the game about speed. If you can't compete with a company's product development, make the game about services you can provide. If you can't compete with another school's technology, make the game about the quality of the teachers you hire. If you can't compete in the market, find a new market you can compete in , or create your own market. ***Don't play by the rules, make the rules.*** Change the game; don't let the game change you!

> ***LESSON LEARNED:*** *An effective leader ensures that his team has the advantage. If you can't compete in the arena currently contested, transform the arena into one more comfortable for you and less comfortable for your competition.*

Keith G. Feit

Lesson #12
ASK NOT WHAT YOUR FOLLOWERS CAN DO FOR YOU...

"We, the people, elect leaders not to rule, but to serve."
- Dwight Eisenhower

> "To feel much for others and little for ourselves; to restrain our selfishness and exercise our benevolent affections, constitute the perfection of human nature."
> - Adam Smith

During his inaugural address, President John F. Kennedy told Americans and those around the world that it was time to step up as individuals and contribute to society. In his famous speech, he said,

> "...And so my fellow Americans, ask not what your country can do for you, ask what you can do for your country. My fellow citizens of the world, ask not what America can do for you, but what together we can do for the freedom of man."

Much as Kennedy told the world, leaders must have the understanding that their position as leader is not a free pass to simply ask more and more from their followers. Leadership is about influencing the direction of followers. Leadership is also about serving followers. Just as President Kennedy challenged Americans to serve their nation and the world, organizations challenge leaders to serve their followers and the organization, itself. Servant leadership has become a popular theory recently, but I am not going to get into a theoretical discussion of its value. Rather, I would prefer to suggest that leadership is not simply about what a leader asks of his or her followers, but also about what he or she can give to his or her followers – inspiration, motivation, support, advice, technical assistance, etc. If I were speaking to a group of leaders today, I might lean on JFK's inaugural and finish by challenging the group to... *"**Ask not what your followers can do for you, but what you can do in service to your followers. To your followers, ask not what the organization can do for them, but what together leader and follower can do to achieve our goals."***

In perusing leadership material one day, I came across the 15five blog, and a post by David Mizne, titled, *"The New Leadership Paradigm."* This interesting picture was presented:

Figure 2. New Paradigm of Leadership

Be A Bean!

This perfectly sums up the purpose of this lesson… an effective leader is one who is willing to get down in the trenches with his followers. As General George Patton once said, "Always do everything you ask of those you command." A leader is not merely a manager supervising a collection of employees, ensuring that they are following procedures and accomplishing tasks. A leader actively engages with followers. A leader lives by the creed, "I will not ask you to do anything I wouldn't be willing to do myself," and then proceeds to back up words with action. When followers work with a leader, rather than for him or her, they attack the task with commitment, and are inspired and motivated to go above and beyond to accomplish the leader's, and organization's, goals. When followers work for a leader, or under a boss, then they are more likely to work out of compliance, limiting their effort to only that which they must give to preserve their position within the organization.

> "As we look ahead into the next century, leaders will be those who empower others."
>
> - Bill Gates,
> Founder of Microsoft and Gates Foundation

One of the interesting texts I came across in my research of servant leadership was found at www.agiftofinspiration.com in the form of Michael Josephson's, *Parable of Brother Leo*:

> *A legend tells of a French monastery known throughout Europe for the extraordinary leadership of a man known only as Brother Leo.*
>
> *Several monks began a pilgrimage to visit Brother Leo to learn from him. Almost immediately, they*

began to bicker about who should do various chores.

On the third day they met another monk going to the monastery, and he joined them. This monk never complained or shirked a duty, and whenever the others would fight over a chore, he would gracefully volunteer and do it himself.

By the last day, the others were following his example, and from then on, they worked together smoothly.

When they reached the monastery, and asked to see Brother Leo, the man who greeted them laughed.

'But our brother is among you!' And he pointed to the fellow who had joined them.

We see here that leadership does not come from a position, but from how an individual behaves. The monks did not know they were in the presence of Brother Leo, yet his actions led them all to become more productive and accomplish their tasks without disagreement. By involving himself in the most mundane of tasks, without hesitation and without complaint, Brother Leo inspired the others to do the same. This was the power of Brother Leo's leadership. This is why his leadership was known to be

> *"A leader... is like a shepherd. He stays behind the flock, letting the most nimble got out ahead, where upon the others follow, not realizing that all along they are being directed from behind."*
>
> - Nelson Mandela

exceptional throughout the world. This is how he was able to move people in the same direction without a position of authority. He did not engender the trust and loyalty from other monks due to his position of authority or the orders he barked, but rather from his willingness to get down and dirty with others. He did not ask the other monks to do what he, himself, was not willing to do. This is the essence of leadership – it doesn't come from position or rank, it comes from actions. As Josephson states, Brother Leo comes from a place "…where leaders are preoccupied with serving rather than being followed, with giving rather than getting, with doing rather than demanding." Brother Leo was a servant leader.

In the end, for a leader to be effective, he or she must understand that the leader is just a cog in the machine of the organization, albeit a very important cog. Alone, the leader cannot succeed, and without the leader, the organization cannot succeed. Leader and follower must work as one for the organization to succeed and thrive. Regardless of a leader's efforts, it is the work of the organization's membership that will lead the way into the future, much the way President Kennedy laid the success or failure of our nation squarely on the shoulders of the citizenry, when during his inauguration he challenged the nation to step up to civic duty. Leaders should learn to heed Kennedy's words, *"In your hands, my fellow citizens, more than mine, will rest the final success or failure of our course."*

LESSON LEARNED: *Leadership is not telling people what to do and watching them attempt to do it; leadership is getting down in the trenches with supporters and working with them to achieve the goal.*

Keith G. Feit

Be A Bean!

Lesson #13
THE ONLY THING YOU HAVE TO FEAR...

> *"I learned that courage was not the absence of fear, but the triumph over it. The brave man is not he who does not feel afraid, but he who conquers that fear."*
> – Nelson Mandela

U.S. President Franklin Roosevelt, during the great depression, once said:

> *"So, first of all, let me assert my firm belief that the only thing we have to fear is...fear itself —— nameless, unreasoning, unjustified terror which paralyzes needed efforts to convert retreat into advance."*

Let's think about that... the only thing we have to fear, is fear itself. We have to fear being afraid. We have to fear the fear of making mistakes. We have to fear the fear of being wrong, of being different, of thinking and acting differently, of challenging conventional wisdom and the status quo. Fear of any of these aforementioned things does exactly what Roosevelt warns, it paralyzes our efforts to advance. We cannot be afraid to take a chance, to risk failure in efforts to advance our current situation.

Failure in such efforts does not end the pursuit of success, but the fear of making such efforts will most certainly prevent us from reaching our preferred destination.

Nelson Mandela, Mark Twain, and many other notable figures throughout history have similar feelings regarding fear. Being strong, being brave, displaying courage are not about being fearless. An individual who is fearless is insane! All human beings fear things, whether it be certain animals, specific situations, particular individuals etc. We are all afraid. The key to being an effective leader, as well as the key to a happy, successful life, is not to avoid fear, but to attack it head on. If you wish to succeed, and you wish to lead others, you need to master your fear.

How does one master fear? First and foremost, you must acknowledge the fear exists. To deny the fear is to ensure its continued hold over your life and the outcomes of your thoughts, words, and actions. Once you have acknowledged your fear, you must put yourself in situations in which you are forced to face the fear. Only if you experience the fear can you learn to overcome its potent paralysis. As you put yourself in situations where the fear exists, you must learn from how you interact with the fear. Learn how to harness your emotions, what you do that alleviates the grip of the fear and what you need to avoid that tightens its grip on your reality. Along this process, two factors are critical to successfully mastering your fear. First is attitude. You must be open to leaving your comfort zone, positive in your ability to overcome your fear, and absolute in your desire to succeed. Along with a fear-busting attitude, you have to open your mind to visualizing the positive outcome when you successfully master your fear. Think not of what the object of your fear can do to stifle your success, but rather what success will look like when you successfully conquer your fear.

> *"Courage is resistance to fear, mastery of fear, not absence of fear."*
>
> - Mark Twain

What does this mastering of fear look like? If you fear public speaking, take as many opportunities as you can to speak in front of people, whether it be addressing a family reunion, telling a story to a group of colleagues, giving a speech to motivate employees, etc. Do not avoid such situations, but embrace them. Actually, seek them out. Each time you have such an opportunity, reflect on the event. Think about what went well. Find out what worked and what didn't work. Try to eliminate those things that increased the fear or anxiety. Throughout any speaking engagement, remain positive and visualize the outcome you desire - the applause at the end of a speech, the laughs at the end of a joke, etc. As you move from one experience to the next, your fear should lessen, until you have finally mastered the fear.

I suffered from a tremendous fear of public speaking, so much so that I avoided social gatherings, failed assignments requiring presentations, and attempted at all costs to remain hidden in class. In fact, I often stuttered or hesitated when speaking in front of a group of people. I had no desire to participate in any such situations. It was only by accident that I mastered my fear, but I learned why I successfully conquered my fear of public speaking. I still get nervous, but actually enjoy giving speeches to large groups of people. I began coaching, and as anyone who has coached knows, communication is critical to the success of a team. I began giving pre-game pep talks, post-game speeches, and speaking in front of groups came a little easier, but the fear was still there. I learned that thinking about screwing up made me anxious, so I began to envision nothing but success. I then entered the PhD program in Educational Leadership and in seminar-like classes, hiding was not an option. I was forced to participate in class discussions, in front of peers who always seemed more intelligent and more educated than I. I learned to be myself and introduce humor in my comments, honestly share my thoughts, and as I participated more, I grew more comfortable. Then, as athletic director, I had to speak in front of hundreds of people at our annual sports banquets. I dreaded each of these moments. I wanted to call out sick, but that wasn't an option, as my assistant would have

> *"Inaction breeds doubt and fear. Action breeds confidence and courage. If you want to conquer fear, do not sit home and think about it. Go out and get busy."*
>
> - Dale Carnegie

killed me! I got up on stage, sweat profusely, made my errors, and continued to grind out every speech. Then, it happened... My fear was gone and I not only did not dread speaking at the banquet, I actually volunteered to give the keynote addresses. I did so, and the reviews from parents and students in attendance were glowingly positive, with many parents requesting copies of the video of the speeches. I have mastered the fear of public speaking, and have now grown to enjoy the opportunity to give a good speech.

General George Patton once said,

> *"Battle is the most magnificent competition in which a human being can indulge. It brings out all that is best; it removes all that is base. All men are afraid in battle. The coward is the one who lets his fear overcome his sense of duty."*

As a leader, it is your duty to lead your family, team, or organization to success. Attainment of your common goals is the ultimate measure of successful leadership, which requires not only the development, but also the communication of a desirable vision of the future, strategies for aligning the entire organization and its members in the same direction in pursuit of the goals, and execution of decisions and actions that lead to progress in that direction. Fear of making the wrong decision, failing, angering others... these are all realistic human emotions. An effective leader overcomes those fears; a poor leader is paralyzed by them. Patton's words ring true... ***a leader who fears failure is a coward, and not worthy of followers' respect, trust, and loyalty.***

> *"Our doubts are traitors and make us lose the good we oft might win by fearing to attempt."*
> - William Shakespeare

Master your fear or be paralyzed by indecision, trepidation, and lack of progress. Be proactive and attack your fears; reacting to fear rather than getting out in front of it grows the fear and strengthens its hold over who you are and how you behave.

Be A Bean!

Conquer your fear or let your fear conquer you!

> **LESSON LEARNED:** *Do not be afraid to stand alone, do not fear being different, do not fear failure…the only thing a leader should fear is not having the courage to take a chance.*

Keith G. Feit

Lesson #14
KNOW WHEN TO LEAD AND WHEN TO FOLLOW

"Don't walk behind me, I may not lead."
- Louisa May Alcott

"A wise old owl sat on an oak; The more he saw the less he spoke. The less he spoke the more he heard; Why aren't we like that wise old owl?"
- Edward Hershey Richards

A leader knows when to speak and when to listen…When to command and when to request…When to stand up and lead, and when to sit down and follow. Being a leader does not mean being the only voice that is ever heard, or being the final say on every decision. Being a leader is more about knowing when others have a better idea, a better solution, or a better strategy. The most important job of a leader is bringing the right people into the organization, and letting them play to their strengths. An effective leader allows his followers to "do their thing" with the least amount of interference possible. Why? It's simple – because a leader believes in his or her judgment, and a leader puts followers in positions where they will be most successful.

During my career, I have not had the best luck

> *"Courage is what it takes to stand up and speak; courage is also what it takes to sit down and listen."*
>
> - Winston Churchill, British Prime Minister

with the administrators with whom I have had to work. In fact, a big part of the problem was that these administrators seemed to believe that the teachers worked for them, not with them. We were two distinct teams, rather than one team working for the betterment of the students. However, there was one administrator that I learned a lot from. There were two major things she taught me. The first was to break all the rules, and while I stated earlier that I think leadership is not about breaking the rules, but more about making the rules, it was an important lesson that forced me to think about playing it safe and simply following orders. The second, and the one that has led to this lesson, is that a leader doesn't do anything that a follower can do better. Delegating is a critical skill of an effective leader – not to reduce the leader's workload but to find a way to accomplish the work more effectively. If someone on the team or within the organization is better at something, why not let them do it? Pride should never get in the way of ensuring the task gets done most efficiently and most effectively.

When I took over the K-12 athletics program, the first thing I did was to determine what tasks needed to be accomplished. I hired two assistant athletic directors and proceeded to delegate responsibilities within the department to each of my assistants. Once I delegated, I removed myself from the equation, except to make sure that all tasks were accomplished. I refuse to delegate and then micromanage. If I hire someone to do a job, then my responsibility as a leader is to respect his or her ability to do the job, and to stay out of the way. This may mean that I become a follower and allow my assistant to lead in that area of responsibility, and this is what I try to do. For example, one of my assistants was extremely capable in organizing special events, and was therefore delegated the responsibility of organizing the annual sports banquets at the end of the school year. My role – whatever she told me I needed to do. It turned out that I created the presentation and program for the event while she handled all the logistics. When it came to the

> *"Don't walk behind me; I may not lead. Don't walk in front of me; I may not follow. Just walk beside me and be my friend."*
>
> - Albert Camus

Be A Bean!

sports banquet, she was the leader and I was the follower, and there was no question as to the relationship. The result… fantastic events that consistently received praise from those that attended. My assistant did a fantastic job as a leader, and hopefully she feels I did a pretty good job as a follower.

Nelson Mandela, widely acknowledged as one of the greatest leaders in world history, struggled through decades in prison for standing up against the racist system of apartheid that allowed a white minority to control a predominantly black country in South Africa. Mandela fought for the rights of his people, refusing to be quieted even when faced when a lifetime in prison. He became the symbol of the movement, and the apartheid system was eventually abolished as free elections were finally held in South Africa. Freed from prison and the most well-known voice of opposition led Nelson Mandela to victory in the presidential race. This highly-respected freedom fighter and political leader once said,

> *"It is better to lead from behind and to put others in front, especially when you celebrate victory when nice things occur. You take the front line when there is danger. Then people will appreciate your leadership."*

Leadership is not always about being in the front of the line and taking credit for victories, and should never be about self-promotion. I have to deal with leaders in my profession who are self-promoters, people who like to advance themselves in the community as servant leaders, but are actually what my mentor termed, **"Self-servant"** leaders. I have seen this type of individual quickly lose the respect of their subordinates, resulting in work completed out of compliance rather than commitment. The result is always clear… the

> *"A leader is best when people barely know he exists, when his work is done, his aim fulfilled, they will say: we did it ourselves."*
>
> - Lao Tzu

students, whom we serve, are let down. Don't misunderstand what I am saying; I have always been fortunate to work with masterful teachers, many of whom are far superior teachers than I. These consummate professionals have always worked seriously and given their best efforts to provide the highest quality educational services for our students. What I am saying is that leadership has often been a barrier, rather than a bridge, to success.

Why are we mentioning these self-servant leaders? We mention them here because these are the leaders who are first in line to claim credit for successes and the first to lay blame for failures. When there is danger, these individuals run for cover and leave their people to face it alone – cower to parents rather than defend teachers, settle a lawsuit rather than fight against unjust allegations, demote or terminate an employee to satisfy an unhappy customer, etc. They are also reactionary, waiting until there is no choice but to address an issue rather than having the courage to proactively head off the trouble or face potential trouble before the negative impact grows. Rather than lead from behind and allow others to receive credit for successes, and stand tall and accept responsibility for failures, shielding subordinates from damaging consequences, these individuals serve only their own personal interests. Rarely does such a leader transform a team or organization, and even less common is sustained success achieved under such leadership. Sometimes the best leadership is unseen; sometimes the best leadership is following someone else's lead. *To be a truly effective leader, one must know when to lead, when to follow, and when they should just get the heck out of the way!*

> LESSON LEARNED: *A true leader actively listens to others, heeds advice, and is open to ideas that are not his or her own. The effective leader also understands that the best leadership is often following the lead of others.*

Lesson #15
CHALLENGES – BARRIERS, OBSTACLES, OR OPPORTUNITIES?

"Veni. Vidi. Vici."
("I came. I saw. I conquered.")
– Julius Caesar

"A pessimist sees the difficulty in every opportunity; an optimist sees the opportunity in every difficulty"
– Sir Winston Churchill

"I love to win; but I love to lose almost as much. I love the thrill of victory, and I also love the challenge of defeat." What a strange quote… how can someone love defeat? This quote comes from one of the greatest baseball players of all-time, Lou Gehrig, who played 1st base for the famed New York Yankees. If one knows the story of Lou Gehrig, and the grace he displayed when facing the debilitating disease named after him, it is not too much of a stretch to understand his thought. Gehrig embraced challenges as opportunities. If he struck out, he learned from the at-bat, and went back out to get on base the next plate appearance. Defeat was an opportunity to right what was wrong, to learn lessons about why he was defeated, so that he can improve upon the weaknesses and succeed even greater later. A loss in the season is invaluable if the team learns enough to win in the playoffs.

Life is full of hills and valleys, and bumps along the way. It is a roller coaster ride of ups and downs, and one of the most important questions one can ask of a leader is – How does he/she respond to the downs in life? Getting knocked down is not embarrassing, it happens to us all. Whether or not we cower and back down after getting knocked to the ground or get up and fight is what separates leaders from followers.

In World War II, when all that stood between Adolf Hitler and Nazi domination of Europe was the tiny island nation of Great Britain, the British Prime Minister, Winston Churchill, held the fate of Western civilization in his hand. As he said to the British Parliament on June 18, 1940, in one of the most famous speeches in history,

> *"Hitler knows that he will have to break us in this island or lose the war. If we can stand up to him, all Europe may be free, and the life of the world may move forward into broad, sunlit uplands. But if we fail, then the whole world, including the United States, including all that we have known and cared for, will sink into the abyss of a new Dark Age made more sinister, and perhaps more protracted, by the lights of perverted science."*

The military might of the Nazi war machine was seen by most European leaders to be unstoppable, and the previous British Prime Minister, Neville Chamberlain, along with the leaders of France, tried to avoid confrontation with Hitler at all costs, including allowing the German dictator to simply annex territory belonging to neighboring sovereign nations. Chamberlain was a leader who saw challenges

> *"Accept the challenges so that you can feel the exhilaration of victory."*
>
> - General George S. Patton

as barriers, Churchill saw challenges as opportunities. Whereas Chamberlain saw potential conflict with Germany as a barrier to peace, Churchill viewed the challenge of Great Britain standing alone against Nazi tyranny as an opportunity for the British people to guarantee peace for future generations of all western nations through the defeat of a perverted madman and his followers. He exclaimed, "… if the British Empire and its Commonwealth last for a thousand years, men will still say, this was their finest hour." Chamberlain saw what could be the darkest hour for the British people approaching, while Churchill saw the imminence of their finest hour. The world could be a much different place today if Chamberlain remained Prime Minister rather than Winston Churchill, and if Churchill did not accept challenges as opportunities. The perception of a challenge is a powerful factor in the success of a leader.

How do you view challenges? Do you see a challenge as a barrier, preventing you from your destination? Are challenges simply obstacles that you must avoid in order to achieve your goal? Or are challenges opportunities for victories you might not yet have ventured to entertain?

How do you deal with a challenge? Do you allow the challenge to derail your journey, or do you attack the challenge and continue along? Read the parable below, and think about how you handle challenges:

In ancient times, a king had a boulder placed on a roadway. Then he hid himself and watched to see if anyone would remove the huge rock.

Some of the king's wealthiest merchants and courtiers came by and simply walked around it. Many loudly blamed the king for not keeping the roads clear, but none did anything about getting the stone out of the way.

Then a peasant came along carrying a load of vegetables. Upon approaching the boulder, the peasant laid down his burden and tried to move the stone to the side of the road. After much pushing and straining, he finally succeeded.

After the peasant picked up his load of vegetables, he noticed a purse lying in the road where the boulder had been. The purse contained many gold coins and a note from the king indicating that the gold was for the person who removed the boulder from the roadway. (www.parablesite.com)

The peasant did not see the boulder as an opportunity, except for as an opportunity to continue along his path. However, what he learned, was that every challenge presents an opportunity. If you see challenges as barriers, you quit and are easily defeated. If you see challenges as obstacles that must be overcome, you will most certainly be delayed in your search for your ultimate destination, or pushed off course in attempts to avert the challenge. However, if you see that every challenge presents an opportunity, then you will attack the challenge with diligence and passion, not only allowing you to reach that destination, but also opening opportunities you never realized were there…much like our peasant in the parable.

Challenges are a part of life's journey, and how you approach a challenge tells the story of who you are as a person and as a leader. Some people look at challenges as barriers that

> *"Everything negative – pressure, challenges – is all an opportunity for me to rise."*
>
> - Kobe Bryant

are immovable or unavoidable, and alter their journey due to fear of failing to overcome the adversity, never attempting to tackle it head on. Others, those who are more confident and believe more in their journey, look at challenges not as barriers that present an end, but as obstacles that present the need to find new ways, ways that do not halt the journey, but delay it due to a concern for averting the obstacle. Finally, there are people who do not see obstacles or barriers. They merely see opportunities, opportunities for a new path; perhaps a new beginning; either way, they see an opportunity for something special. These people are those who find greatness along their journey, not because they were born great, but because greatness found them by way of their persistence through all the struggles. *The challenges provided them with opportunities to grow, learn, master their fate, and determine their destination.*

> LESSON LEARNED: *Challenges are not barriers or obstacles, but rather opportunities to find new ways, open new doors, and travel new paths on the road to success.*

Keith G. Feit

Lesson #16
RELATIONSHIPS RULE

"Personal relationships are the fertile soil from which all advancement, all success, all achievement in real life grows."
- Ben Stein

Earlier, we discussed the importance of others in our quest for success, and how it is impossible to find the ultimate success without the support and contributions of others. How does one bring others into his or her crusade, getting them to commit to the goal of the team or organization? RELATIONSHIPS!

President Franklin Roosevelt stressed the importance of developing relationships when he said, "If civilization is to survive, we must learn to cultivate the science of human relationships..." Relationships are the key to effective leadership. Communication skills, organizational skills, motivational ability, technical knowledge...none of it matters unless a leader can develop strong interpersonal relationships. The strength of the relationships goes a long way in determining the success of the organization. Why are strong interpersonal relationships so important?

> *"Never above you. Never below you. Always beside you."*
>
> - Walter Winchell

Think about the people for whom you are willing to do anything. Your family, your closest friends… the people with whom you have the strongest interpersonal relationships and for whom you are willing to make the ultimate sacrifice. People work harder for those they care about. They more enthusiastically follow those they trust. They buy in more when they have a committed loyalty to the person making the decisions. They are always willing to listen to someone they respect. They are willing to sacrifice greatly for those they love. They are willing to run through a wall for someone they trust and who they know cares about them. In the words of General Colin Powell, former Secretary of State and Chairman of the Joint Chiefs of Staff for the U.S. Armed Forces,

> *"The day soldiers stop bringing you their problems is the day you have stopped leading them. They have either lost confidence that you can help them or concluded that you do not care. Either case is a failure of leadership."*

A successful leader has the ability to get his or her message across to others, to persuade others to perceive the goal as a common goal and to pursue that goal with fervor, and to motivate and inspire them to work harder than they thought they could. An individual who succeeds as a leader is one who is able to earn the trust, loyalty, and respect of the membership, assuring each member that every individual within the organization is valued, and the welfare of each member, not just the good of the organization, is a priority of the leadership. The roadmap to success lies in the relationships a leader is able to cultivate.

> *"Nobody cares how much you know, until they know how much you care."*
>
> - President Theodore Roosevelt

> *"Friends show their love in times of trouble, not in happiness."*
>
> - Euripedes

The Bible tells us, "Greater love hath no man than this, that a man lay down his life for his friends." I have had some relationships, outside of family, for which this could not have been any truer. There have been players, students, friends, and assistant coaches who have been "family" to me, and for these people there isn't anything I wouldn't do. I fully gave my heart to some of these individuals believing that the relationships cultivated were true, strong, and the bonds were unbreakable. This leads to a mini-lesson within the "Relationships Rule" lesson... Be sure the relationships you cultivate are true and two-way. Unfortunately, I learned the hard way that only the strongest of relationships are impervious to external pressures such as adversity, the whispers of others, and the lure of immediate gratification. While only the strongest relationships survive adversity, it is only through the presence of adversity that we can judge the strength of the relationship. Adversity is the true test of a relationship... the relationship that remains true through adversity has passed the test. These are the people that you should trust and lean on.

> LESSON LEARNED: *A leader can have positional power, expert power, and unlimited resources, but without strong relationships that engender trust, respect, loyalty, and love, he or she is truly powerless to affect change.*

Keith G. Feit

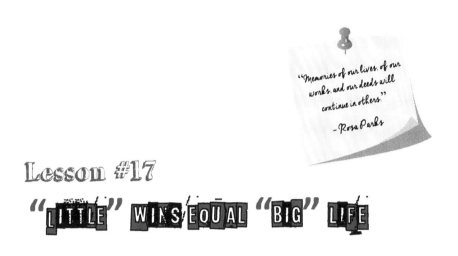

"Memories of our lives, of our works, and our deeds will continue in others."
- Rosa Parks

Lesson #17
"LITTLE" WINS EQUAL "BIG" LIFE

"Very little is needed to make a happy life; it is all within yourself, in your way of thinking."
- Marcus Aurelius

    The key to a good life is the same as the key to good leadership – care about others, be as selfless as possible, don't dwell in the past, create your own future, and determine your own destiny. It is actually very simple to lead a good life. All you need to do is enjoy the little wins in life. The little wins are those things we usually take for granted – loving family, good friends, special relationships, great memories… all those things that bring us happiness so regularly that we neglect to think about them and how lucky we are to have them. Every hug from a loved one, every smile from a friend, every laugh and every tear shared with special others… these are the things that make life special. These are the moments to remember and to treasure.

    This is not to say that big wins are not important. We obviously have goals, and big things we want to accomplish, and these are extremely important. The key is to go after those big wins while enjoying all the little wins along the way. Marriage is a huge part of an individual's life, at least for most people. It is a big win, especially for those who have found the right person and get to live the rest of their life with the person they love. However, marriage is the destination, but what about the journey to get there. How many boyfriends or girlfriends were there along the way, some of with whom the lucky man or woman probably had some memorable experiences? How much did he or she learn from those ultimately unsuccessful experiences that helped lead the individual to the successful relationship he or she finally found? If not for the ex-boyfriend or ex-girlfriend, he or she may not have realized the need for change in order to make his or her significant other happy. Along with the learning from those failed relationships, how many friends were made along the way to finding the right person? How many successes and memorable experiences arose in the individual's professional life? If marriage was the only thing the person thought about and the only concern was to tie the knot, then the individual is missing out on so many of the little things that make life worth living.

As a teacher, we want all of our students to be successful and for our kids to score the highest on the standardized tests that are the basis of our annual evaluations. However, when a teacher looks back on life, is he or she going to remember that 80% of their students in 2017 were proficient in reading, or will he or she remember the one student from a broken home with a learning disability and no hope for a brighter future that went to college because of the inspiration, motivation, and support the teacher gave that student? Will the teacher remember the test score or the special relationship developed, and the special moment realized when he or she watches the student walk across the stage at a college graduation ceremony? A coach strives to win championships, but what about the buzzer beater in the playoffs that led to the championship game, and the instant when the players were jumping up and down, hugging each other, and sharing smiles, laughs, and tears of joy in that moment…what means more, the trophy or that moment? I would trade every trophy I have ever earned for one of

> *"Take care of all your memories, for you cannot relive them."*
>
> - Bob Dylan, American Musician

Be A Bean!

those moments of seeing sheer joy on my players faces and the excitement they shared when the return on their investment of hard work finally came through.

When my basketball team won the championship in a national tournament, I don't remember the trophy presentation. I don't have a clue to what the trophy even looks like. I remember the final buzzer, the players running into the corner of the court jumping on top of each other, the embrace of every player on that team, the smiles on their faces, and the stories, jokes, and happiness on the plane ride home. For me, in that moment, those little wins were priceless, and those little wins are the moments we should always strive for, recognize, and cherish.

Below is a parable from www.parablesite.com that teaches us that what we view as good, could be bad; what we see as big could be small; those things we see as important could actually matter little, and vice versa. Think about what you think is important to you as you read:

> *One day a wealthy father took his son on a trip to the country so that the son could see how the poor lived. They spent a day and a night at the farm of a very poor family.*
>
> *When they got back from their trip, the father asked his son, "How was the trip?"*
>
> *"Very good, Dad!"*
>
> *"Did you see how poor people can be?"*
>
> *"Yeah!"*
>
> *"And what did you learn?"*
>
> *The son answered, "I saw that we have a dog at home, and they have four. We have a pool that reaches to the middle of the garden; they have a creek that has no end. We have imported lamps in*

the house; they have the stars. Our patio reaches to the front yard; they have the whole horizon."

When the little boy was finished, the father was speechless. His son then added, "Thanks Dad for showing me how poor we are!"

The young boy realized that the poor people were leading "big" lives. You do not have to be wealthy or successful to lead a good life. Anyone, regardless of social status, wealth, or profession can learn to appreciate the little things in life, and enjoy every moment of the short time we spend on earth.

When the time comes and your stay on this earth has expired, how will you look back on life? Will you be able to look back at all the smiles, the laughs, the tears, the hugs, the kisses… and reminisce about the great life you lived, or will you look back only at the big successes in life and realize that you lived nothing more than a superficial life? Take the time to enjoy life's little wins; every single one is precious. Don't be the dad who misses his son's baseball game because he had to work late, or the mom who chose to play tennis rather than spend time with her daughter. Don't be afraid to share a hug with a friend, or cry with a loved one. Life is short; whether it is sweet or not depends on the decisions you make and the priorities you set. ***Sometimes it is the littlest things in life that bring about the biggest joys.***

> LESSON LEARNED: ***Life is about the little wins along the journey… relationships developed, friendships made, lives impacted.***

Lesson #18
EMBRACE ADVERSITY

"Difficulties are meant to arouse, not discourage. The human spirit is to grow strong by conflict."
- William Ellery Channing

"Character cannot be developed in ease and quiet. Only through experience of trial and suffering can the soul be strengthened, ambition inspired, and success achieved."
- Helen Keller

If ever, in the course of human history, one man has faced adversity greater than most mortal men can handle, it was Winston Churchill, who was appointed Prime Minister of Great Britain as Adolf Hitler and the Nazi scourge spread its vile culture forcibly across Europe. Yet, in the face of all adversity, Churchill never wavered. Despite the fall of every of his Western European allies, including France, the United States remaining on the sidelines, and the entire might of the German juggernaut with a focused gaze upon the British Isles, Churchill embraced the opportunity to lead. He stood alone, not only within

> *"All life demands struggle. Those who have everything given to them become lazy, selfish, and insensitive to the real values of life. The very striving and hard work that we so constantly try to avoid is the major building block in the person we are today."*
>
> - Pope Paul VI

the international community, but also within his own government, fighting a war for survival. The fate of an entire civilization potentially hung in the balance, Churchill's unwavering confidence all that stood between freedom and Nazi domination. His words inspired a nation while his actions inspired a world. Churchill's bold philosophy on handling adversity can be summed up in his own words,

> *"One ought never to turn one's back on a threatened danger and try to run away from it. If you do that, you will double the danger. But if you meet it promptly and without flinching, you will reduce the danger by half. Never run away from anything. Never!"*

Another famous leader professed his embrace of a potential threat in his presidential inaugural address in 1961. John F. Kennedy exclaimed,

> *"In the long history of the world, only a few generations have been granted the role of defending freedom in its hour of maximum danger. I do not shrink from this responsibility--I welcome it. I do not believe that any of us would exchange places with any other people or any other generation. The energy, the faith, the devotion which we bring to this endeavor will light our country and all who serve it--and the glow from that fire can truly light the world."*

President Kennedy is embracing the adversity that comes from the danger he faces as president, and the United States and western world face from the nuclear showdown with the Soviet Union. He understands that the future is riddled with potential threats to peace, but he confidently announces to the nation and the world that we will not shrink from the challenge. To the contrary, we will rise to meet the challenge with fierce dedication and unbridled energy to ensure that all people, American and non-American alike, are guaranteed a better world.

Adversity affects us all, whether in our social lives with romantic relationships and friendships, professionally with layoffs and firings, or any other aspect of life. Even the greatest among us are not immune to the hardship of adversity. Take Steve Jobs, for example, The Apple icon who is most famous for the creation of the iPod, Ipad, and iPhone, who revolutionized technology and gave rise to the era of smart technology, was forced to become a master of adversity before passing away as a business and technology legend. He was fired from Apple, the company he started. His new business venture, NeXT computer was a miserable failure. The Apple III, Powermac g4 cube, and Apple Lisa were among the products that failed. Despite these setbacks, Jobs learned and continued to innovate.

> "The ultimate measure of a man is not where he stands in moments of comfort and convenience, but where he stands at times of challenge and controversy."
>
> - Rev. Martin Luther King, Jr.

It is adversity that makes us stronger, wiser, braver... without adversity we are never tested, and can never realize our true greatness. Martin Luther King, Jr. advocates for measuring the worth of a man by how he acts when adversity knocks on his door. Any man or woman can act like a leader when things are going well, but true leaders can stand up and lead when it appears the world is crashing down around them. As Helen Keller said, it is our trials and tribulations that determine our character. For a leader, adversity presents an opportunity for motivation and inspiration. If effectively utilized, adversity can work as a uniting force and rally followers to support the leader with a fervent enthusiasm.

I'd like to leave you with this short parable from www.parablesite.com that offers a glimpse into the importance of adversity in our lives:

A man found a cocoon of a butterfly. One day a small opening appeared.

He sat and watched the butterfly for several hours as it struggled to squeeze its body through the tiny hole. Then it stopped, as if it couldn't go further.

So the man decided to help the butterfly. He took a pair of scissors and snipped off the remaining bits of cocoon. The butterfly emerged easily but it had a swollen body and shriveled wings.

The man continued to watch it, expecting that any minute the wings would enlarge and expand enough to support the body... Neither happened! In fact the butterfly spent the rest of its life crawling around. It was never able to fly.

What the man in his kindness and haste did not understand: The restricting cocoon and the struggle required by the butterfly to get through the opening was a way of forcing the fluid from the body into the wings so that it would be ready
for flight once that was achieved.

Sometimes struggles are exactly what we need in our lives. Going through life with no obstacles would cripple us. We will not be as strong as we could have been and we would never fly.

> **LESSON LEARNED:** *Adversity is not the enemy of a leader, but is in fact his or her best friend. Adversity builds character and strengthens both individuals and organizations, and provides a leader an opportunity to earn the trust, admiration, and loyalty of followers.*

Keith G. Feit

Be A Bean!

"The past is not ours to recover, but the future is ours to win or lose."
- President Lyndon Johnson

Lesson #19
LEARN FROM THE PAST, LIVE IN THE PRESENT, CREATE THE FUTURE

"The best way to predict the future is to create it."
- Abraham Lincoln

Joel Osteen makes a great point when he talks about your drive home. He notes that while driving in your car, you are faced with a huge windshield allowing you to look out the front of the car, but just a very small rearview mirror to look out the back of the car. It is obviously much more important to see out the front of the car while driving, hence the very large front windshield. This allows us to see where we are going, representing our future. While it is necessary to look through the rearview mirror if changing lanes, there is only so much a driver can gain from looking out back. Looking

> *"History will be kind to me for I intend to write it."*
>
> - Winston Churchill, British Prime Minister

out this mirror shows us where we have been, representing our past. In this aspect, the driving of a car is like the piloting of our life. The past holds value as we can and should learn from it. The present is important as we are currently living in it. The future, however, is where we can take our lives, and there is no limit to how great it can be. If we learn from our past and make wise decisions in the present, then we have the potential to create a truly amazing future.

Notice I said create. It is my firm belief that our future is the future we build for ourselves. Earlier in this book, we discussed the fact that each individual is the master of his or her fate. This makes them the master of their future. As President Abraham Lincoln advised us, we should work to create the future we envision rather than try to predict what is destined to happen to us. We can dwell in the past and condemn ourselves to a future mired in misery, mediocrity, or stagnancy. We can reside solely in the present while failing to recognize potential opportunities and realizing the promise of the future... OR... we can reflect on the past and live in the present with an eye toward the future.

> *"If we open a quarrel between the past and the present, we shall find we have lost the future."*
>
> - Winston Churchill, British Prime Minister

As a leader, it is critical to not only ensure team or organizational success in the present, but to also make decisions that will guarantee success in the future. Leaders who make short-term decisions at the expense of the long-term are condemning the organization and all its members to inevitable decline. A great leader is able to balance the short-term success of the organization with its long-term viability - A once profitable company that goes bankrupt can hardly be called successful; A championship team that goes into a decade of losing cannot be considered a great franchise; An individual cannot be considered healthy if dietary supplements responsible for youthful fitness lead to cancer in middle age.

The lessons are simple – Do not sacrifice tomorrow for today. Do not let yesterday ruin today. Do not let the fear of tomorrow influence actions today. In other words, a leader cannot live in successes of the past nor dwell on yesterday's failures; he or

Be A Bean!

she must reflect on the past, learn from it, and allow it to inform the decisions he or she makes today, making decisions today that will promote success in both the present and the future. A leader should never sacrifice the potential success of the future for the temporary triumph of the present. There is a balance, and *an effective leader is able to use the past to inform the present and create the future.*

> LESSON LEARNED: *Do not dwell in the failures of yesterday or focus on the limitations of today, but pursue the promise of tomorrow.*

Keith G. Feit

Be A Bean!

"Shadows cannot see themselves in the mirror of the sun"

-Eva Person

Lesson #20
A LEADER'S BEST FRIEND

"I desire to conduct the affairs of this administration that if at the end, when I come to lay down the reins of power, I have lost every friend on earth, I shall at least have one friend left, and that friend shall be down inside me."
- President Abraham Lincoln

Aristotle is quoted as saying, "I count him braver who overcomes his desires than him who conquers his enemies; for the hardest victory is over self." U.S. President Harry Truman agrees, stating, "In reading the lives of great men, I found that the first victory they won was over themselves... self-discipline with all of them came first."

The first time I learned of the poem, *The Guy in the Glass*, was Bill Parcell's retirement speech,

"I care not what others think of what I do, but I care very much about what I think of what I do: That is character!"

- President Theodore Roosevelt

following his resignation as head coach of the New York Jets. This was quite a loss for the franchise, a Hall of Fame football coach and the man who had so quickly turned the team into a Super Bowl contender. Parcells could have continued as he was a beloved figure in the New York area thanks to his great success with the New York Giants, including two Super Bowl championships. However, he knew that while he was still a competent football coach, he didn't have the desire to continue the daily grind, and while he easily could have fooled the press and the fans, and to an extent even the players and ownership, he could not fool the guy in the glass. The guy in the glass was telling him it was time, and so he stepped away as head coach.

In Lesson #3, we dealt with the need for leaders to be true to themselves. This pertains to this lesson as well. A leader, while often able to fool many, and maybe most of the people, will never be able to fool him or herself. For some people, it is easier to lie and cheat oneself due to the lack of moral compass or grounding in a strong, value-based foundation. For those people, it is the lure to achieve status, assume power, or obtain riches or fame that drives the individual. This allows them to disregard the disappointment of the man or woman in the glass. It does, however, inhibit their ability to be effective leaders. These individuals usually struggle to develop the strong relationships needed to develop commitment, and totally lack the desire to positively impact anyone's life but their own. For those with strong morals, values, and ethics, it is important to make decisions that are driven by a desire to work for others, help others, and to positively impact followers and the outcomes of the organization. For these leaders, who are much more capable of developing strong professional and personal relationships, the guy or gal in the glass presents a reminder of the person he or she hopes, expects, and needs to be.

If you think about those modern leaders who have led nations through their darkest hours – Abraham Lincoln and the American Civil War; Winston Churchill and World War II; Franklin Roosevelt and the Great Depression; John F. Kennedy, Ronald Reagan and the Cold War – then you see an individual of uncommon self-

> *"When your values are clear to you, making decisions is easy.*
>
> - Roy Disney

Be A Bean!

assuredness in the face of ridicule. Each of these men had to deal not only with external enemies, but also detractors within. Lincoln was mocked throughout his administration, and greater respect was regularly given his cabinet, then the president, himself. Churchill was derided as a drunk and a warmonger. Franklin Roosevelt was stricken with polio and confined mostly to a wheelchair. Kennedy suffered terribly from health issues resulting in part from war injuries, as well as the rumors of his infidelities. Reagan was actually called an "amiable dunce" by the opposition, and his own future vice-president once termed Reagan's economic plan as "voodoo economics." Rather than wilt from the criticism and opposition, these men of strength, courage, and tremendous leadership did not waver from their principles. Despite the struggles, instances of doubt and depression, and many hardships along the way, these men were always able to look in the mirror and proudly recognize the face they saw looking back at them. Each was human, far less than perfect, but each was able to stand tall when lesser men shrunk, and each was able to stand up to the challenges and meet the very high expectations and standards of the man in the glass. Those who are not true to themselves, are unsure of who they are or what they are capable of, who lack the confidence in their ability or the strength to stand up to criticism and dissonance, or those who fail to hold themselves to high standards will always struggle to stand up to the man or woman in the glass. Those are the people who will wither when the pressure rises while those who maintain a strong, positive, relationship with the man or woman in the glass will always be able to rise to the occasion and succeed beyond even their own expectations.

Ernest Hemingway was quoted as saying, "There is nothing noble in being superior to your fellow men. True nobility lies in being superior to your former self." The man or woman in the glass is the measure of how an individual stacks up against his or her former self. The person looking back tells the story of who we have been, who we are, and can inspire us to become who we are destined to be. An individual who can look in the mirror and be proud of the person looking back is an individual who has led a good life, been a leader, and made a positive difference in the world.

> LESSON LEARNED: *The only approval an individual needs is internal… one must be able to look in the mirror and be satisfied with the life he or she has chosen to lead.*

Be A Bean!

"THE GUY IN THE GLASS"

When you get what you want in your struggle for pelf,
And the world makes you King for a day,
Then go to the mirror and look at yourself,
And see what that guy has to say.

For it isn't your Father, or Mother, or Wife,
Whose judgment upon you must pass.
The feller whose verdict counts most in your life
Is the guy staring back from the glass.

He's the feller to please, never mind all the rest,
For he's with you clear up to the end,
And you've passed your most dangerous, difficult test
If the guy in the glass is your friend.

You may be like Jack Horner and "chisel" a plum,
And think you're a wonderful guy,
But the man in the glass says you're only a bum
If you can't look him straight in the eye.

You can fool the whole world down the pathway of years,
And get pats on the back as you pass,
But your final reward will be heartaches and tears
If you've cheated the guy in the glass.

- Dale Wimbrow (c. 1934)

Keith G. Feit

Be A Bean!

Culminating Lesson
ENJOY THE JOURNEY

"Character is a journey, not a destination."
— President Bill Clinton

Earlier I wrote about standing on the shoulders of giants. One of those giants in my life, and a giant in the educational leadership profession, was my doctoral mentor and dissertation chair, Dr. John Pisapia. When we lost Dr. Pisapia, I had to come to grips with the fact that I would never have that undying support, mentorship, and love again. What I will have forever are all the lessons he taught me while I was fortunate enough to have him by my side. The greatest lesson of all is also one of the simplest – Enjoy the Journey.

Pursuing perfection is not a short-term activity, but rather a long, arduous journey. This adventure called life, and each mini-venture we pursue, are all roller coaster rides of conflicting emotions... anticipation and fright, satisfaction and disappointment, elation and despair. Those who are wise understand what tennis legend Arthur Ashe meant when he said, "Success is a journey, not a destination. The doing is often more important than the outcome."

> *"Enjoy the journey and try to get better every day. And don't lose the passion and love for what you do."*
>
> — Nadia Comaneci,
> (Olympic Gold Medalist)

We often close our eyes and minds along the way to reaching our goals, only allowing ourselves to imagine the thrill of victory we expect, the satisfaction of the ultimate success at the end of the journey. After all, the championship trophy at the end of a season, the "A" at the end of the school semester, the client signing on at the end of a pursuit, or reaching number one on the bestseller list after publishing a novel... those are all that matter, right? Who pays attention to the losses throughout the season, the B's and C's on tests and papers, the mistakes made in developing relationships during the client pursuit, or the moments of writer's block and numerous revisions during the writing process? Why should we actually take a moment to learn from our mistakes in the failures of our endeavors in pursuit of our desired outcome?

Unfortunately, that is the attitude of most people, most of the time. Get to the destination as quickly as possible, failing to take notice of most of the journey. I made this mistake most of my life. As a coach, the only thing I worried about was winning the championship, about being recognized as the best at the end of every season. Every day, my ultimate goal blinded me to everything I was missing in life; the little victories that are often overshadowed by the big prize. Unlike that championship trophy or "A" in the class, the client signing on, or the recognition of being a bestseller, the "little" wins are the "big" things that stay with us for life – they are the relationships we develop, the laughs we share with others, the tears we shed alongside those that matter most. This is what life is about. This is also the essence of leadership. Life, and leadership, are about the journey, not the destination. It is along the journey that mistakes happen, learning occurs, friendships are made, love is found, and the tools of success are nurtured. The journey is where we become who we really are; in fact, the journey makes us who we are.

Think about it... we never find perfection, do we? That would mean we never reach the ultimate destination. But in the end, it is the journey, the pursuit of perfection, that leads us to excellence. If excellence in everything we do is our final destination, as it should be, then what we do throughout the pursuit will determine whether or not we get there. Repeating those things that led to excellence, and eliminating those things that led to failure, will lead to continued success. Simply put, to continue to be successful, we must continue those things that we learned worked along the journey, and adjust those things that didn't work.

It was the journey in my PhD program, and not the doctoral degree I received at the end, that led to my close relationship with a great person, and memories and lessons that will carry me through life forever. The degree has not made me a better leader; the lessons I learned from Dr. Pisapia, my other professors, my peers, and my experiences along the journey have most certainly made me a better leader. They have also made me a better person.

I will miss Dr. Pisapia every day for the rest of my life – every time I step in a classroom, read an article, or make a leadership decision; he is irreplaceable and unforgettable. He is now part of who I am and who I will become. I will always remember how he lived his life and the major lesson he imparted on me - Regardless of where your adventure ends and who follows you in those pursuits, learn to truly live life, lead as a lifelong learner, and be sure to always enjoy the journey.

> LESSON LEARNED: *Life is short; respect & appreciate every precious moment. Celebrate the good, learn from the bad, reflect on all. Wherever life takes you, enjoy the journey!*

Keith G. Feit

Be A Bean!

Feit's Final Thoughts...

"I am not afraid of an army of lions led by sheep. I am afraid of an army of sheep led by a lion."
- Alexander the Great

"Be true to yourself, help others, make each day your masterpiece, make friendship a fine art, drink deeply from good books - especially the Bible, build a shelter against a rainy day, give thanks for your blessings and pray for guidance every day."
- John Wooden

Be true to who you are, not who others expect you to be. Be a person that lives by high standards and sets lofty goals. Be a person that takes chances and does not fear failure. Be a person who, regardless of what target you chase, always pursues perfection. Be a person who strives to be a force for good, speaks to others' hopes and dreams, stands up for all, does what is right and just, remains bold in words and actions, and accepts the responsibility as the master of your own fate. Embrace adversity as the engine of greatness, celebrate failure as the foundation to success, and contemplate challenges as opportunities to accomplish amazing things.

Do not react to environmental changes, but rather proactively engage the environment to make it work for you. Do not let the world dictate who you are; you figure out who you are and then proudly go out and conquer the world.

Be your own person, follow your own heart, speak your own words, live your own life...

Let this be the philosophy that guides you through life – be a better son or daughter, be a better brother or sister, be a better friend, a better teammate, a better leader... most importantly, be a better person. Always strive to be the best person you can be and to have the greatest positive impact you can possibly have. Leave your family better, your team better, your organization better, your community better, and in some small way, leave the world a better place because you were a part of it.

If you live that life, if you are guided by such a philosophy, then you will achieve excellence, and others will prosper because you led. Whatever you do, always be sure to make the person in the mirror proud. After all, you are the one who determines whether your coin has heads on both sides... you determine whether you are a carrot, egg, or coffee bean.

BE A BEAN!

Be A Bean!

"Be a yardstick of quality. Some people aren't used to an environment where excellence is expected."
— Steve Jobs

THE 10 COMMANDMENTS OF A LEADER

1. The greater good supersedes individual ambition; always strive to have a positive impact on others in everything you do.

2. Never settle for ordinary when you can be extraordinary; Always think big – Dream it, dare it, do it.

3. Build bridges, not walls. Relationships are the true currency of leadership.

4. When the game doesn't fit your style of play, change the rules and make others play a different game.

5. "Veni, Vidi, Vici" - When adversity rears its ugly head... embrace it, challenge it, and conquer it.

6. Think and act differently; Listening to conventional wisdom is like accepting advice from a fool.

7. Challenge the status quo; It is nothing more than a barrier to reaching beyond the possible and into the impossible.

8. Foster a growth mindset – celebrate failure as a learning experience, promote creativity and innovation in yourself and your organization, and proactively create opportunities.

9. Always make the person in the mirror proud – be true to who you are as a person and leader. Let your heart be your guide as you ignore the whispers of others and always stand up for what is right.

10. Never dwell on the failures of yesterday or constrain yourself to the limits of today, but always pursue the promise of tomorrow.

Be A Bean!

Dr. Keith G. Feit is an educational leadership researcher with a bachelor's degree in biological sciences, and M.Ed. and Ph.D. degrees in educational leadership from Florida Atlantic University. He has been an educator for over 20 years and served in numerous leadership capacities in schools, including Chairman of the School Advisory Body, Team Leader, Teacher on Special Administrative Assignment, Director of Athletics, President of the Faculty Senate, and Chairman of the Discipline Committee, as well as serving as the founding commissioner of a high school athletics conference.

Made in the USA
Las Vegas, NV
12 July 2021